Teach Yourself
VISUALLY™
PhotoShop® Elements 3

Visual™

by Sherry Willard Kinkoph

and Mike Wooldridge

WILEY

Wiley Publishing, Inc.

Teach Yourself VISUALLY™ Photoshop® Elements 3

Published by
Wiley Publishing, Inc.
111 River Street
Hoboken, NJ 07030-5774

Published simultaneously in Canada

Library of Congress Control Number: 2004112348

ISBN-13: 978-0-7645-6912-8

ISBN-10: 0-7645-6912-0

Manufactured in the United States of America

10 9 8 7 6 5 4 3 2 1

Trademark Acknowledgments

Contact Us

For general information on our other products and services please contact our Customer Care Department within the U.S. at 800-762-2974, outside the U.S. at 317-572-3993 or fax 317-572-4002.

For technical support please visit www.wiley.com/techsupport.

WILEY

Wiley Publishing, Inc.

Sales

Contact Wiley
at (800) 762-2974 or
fax (317) 572-4002.

Praise for Visual Books

"Like a lot of other people, I understand things best when I see them visually. Your books really make learning easy and life more fun."

John T. Frey (Cadillac, MI)

"I have quite a few of your Visual books and have been very pleased with all of them. I love the way the lessons are presented!"

Mary Jane Newman (Yorba Linda, CA)

"I just purchased my third Visual book (my first two are dog-eared now!), and, once again, your product has surpassed my expectations.

Tracey Moore (Memphis, TN)

"I am an avid fan of your Visual books. If I need to learn anything, I just buy one of your books and learn the topic it in no time. Wonders! I have even trained my friends to give me Visual books as gifts."

Illona Bergstrom (Aventura, FL)

"Thank you for making it so clear. I appreciate it. I will buy many more Visual books."

J.P. Sangdong (North York, Ontario, Canada)

"I have several books from the Visual series and have always found them to be valuable resources."

Stephen P. Miller (Ballston Spa, NY)

"Thank you for the wonderful books you produce. It wasn't until I was an adult that I discovered how I learn – visually. Nothing compares to Visual books. I love the simple layout. I can just grab a book and use it at my computer, lesson by lesson. And I understand the material! You really know the way I think and learn. Thanks so much!"

Stacey Han (Avondale, AZ)

"I absolutely admire your company's work. Your books are terrific. The format is perfect, especially for visual learners like me. Keep them coming!"

Frederick A. Taylor, Jr. (New Port Richey, FL)

"I have several of your Visual books and they are the best I have ever used."

Stanley Clark (Crawfordville, FL)

"I bought my first Teach Yourself VISUALLY book last month. Wow. Now I want to learn everything in this easy format!"

Tom Vial (New York, NY)

"Thank you, thank you, thank you...for making it so easy for me to break into this high-tech world. I now own four of your books. I recommend them to anyone who is a beginner like myself."

Gay O'Donnell (Calgary, Alberta, Canada)

"I write to extend my thanks and appreciation for your books. They are clear, easy to follow, and straight to the point. Keep up the good work! I bought several of your books and they are just right! No regrets! I will always buy your books because they are the best."

Seward Kollie (Dakar, Senegal)

"Compliments to the chef!! Your books are extraordinary! Or, simply put, extra-ordinary, meaning way above the rest! THANKYOU THANKYOU THANKYOU! I buy them for friends, family, and colleagues."

Christine J. Manfrin (Castle Rock, CO)

"What fantastic teaching books you have produced! Congratulations to you and your staff. You deserve the Nobel Prize in Education in the Software category. Thanks for helping me understand computers."

Bruno Tonon (Melbourne, Australia)

"Over time, I have bought a number of your 'Read Less - Learn More' books. For me, they are THE way to learn anything easily. I learn easiest using your method of teaching."

José A. Mazón (Cuba, NY)

"I am an avid purchaser and reader of the Visual series, and they are the greatest computer books I've seen. The Visual books are perfect for people like myself who enjoy the computer, but want to know how to use it more efficiently. Your books have definitely given me a greater understanding of my computer, and have taught me to use it more effectively. Thank you very much for the hard work, effort, and dedication that you put into this series."

Alex Diaz (Las Vegas, NV)

Credits

Project Editor
Maureen Spears

Acquisitions Editor
Jody Lefevere

Product Development Manager
Lindsay Sandman

Copy Editor
Jerlind Charles

Technical Editor
Dennis Cohen

Editorial Manager
Robyn Siesky

Manufacturing
Allan Conley
Linda Cook
Paul Gilchrist
Jennifer Guynn

Media Development Manager
Laura Carpenter VanWinkle

Permissions Editor
Laura Moss

Proofreader
Christine Pingleton

Indexer
Sherry Massey

Book Design
Kathie S. Rickard

Production Coordinator
Nancee Reeves

Layout
Jennifer Heleine
Amanda Spagnuolo
Erin Zeltner

Screen Artist
Jill A. Proll

Illustrators
Steve Amory
Matthew Bell
Ronda David-Burroughs
Cheryl Grubbs
Sean Johanessen
Jacob Mansfield
Rita Marley
Tyler Roloff

Special Help
Adrienne Porter
Tim Borek

Vice President and Executive Group Publisher
Richard Swadley

Vice President and Publisher
Barry Pruett

Composition Director
Debbie Stailey

About the Authors

Sherry Willard Kinkoph is a freelance author and a fan of all things computer related. She has written over 50 books over the past 10 years covering a variety of computer topics ranging from hardware to software, from Microsoft Office programs to the Internet. Sherry's on-going quest is to help users of all levels master the ever-changing computer technologies.

Mike Wooldridge is a Web developer and author living in the San Francisco Bay Area. This is his thirteenth VISUALLY book.

Together, Sherry and Mike have co-written several titles, including *Master VISUALLY Dreamweaver MX and Flash MX*, and *Master VISUALLY eBay Business Kit*.

Authors' Acknowledgments

Sherry Willard Kinkoph

Special thanks to Barry Pruett and Jody Lefevere for assigning me such a fun book to tackle. Extra special thanks to our editor, Maureen Spears, for her diligence and able guidance throughout the project. Lastly, many gracious thanks to my co-author, Mike Wooldridge, whose humor and talent always make the collaboration process such a pleasurable experience.

Mike Wooldridge

Thanks to Maureen Spears for her careful project editing, Dennis Cohen for his expert technical editing, and Sherry for being a swell co-author. It was enjoyayble working with all of you again.

TABLE OF CONTENTS

 **chapter 1** Getting Started

Introducing Photoshop Elements 3 4

Understanding Digital Images 6

Start Photoshop Elements on a PC 8

The Photoshop Elements PC Workspace 9

Start Photoshop Elements on a Mac 10

The Photoshop Elements Mac Workspace 11

Anatomy of the Elements Toolbox 12

Work with Toolbox Tools 14

Work with Palettes 16

Set Program Preferences 20

Find Help 22

 **chapter 2** Acquiring and Storing Digital Images

Find Images for Your Projects 26

Import Images from a Scanner 28

Import Images from a Digital Camera 30

Import Images from a Card Reader 32

Import Images Using Organizer on a PC 34

Download Images with Adobe Photo Downloader 38

Import Images from a Video 42

Save an Image 44

Close an Image 45

Open an Image 46

Create a New Image 48

chapter 3 Image Basics

Work with Image Windows 52

Magnify with the Zoom Tool 54

Adjust the Image View 56

Change the Image Size 58

Change the Image Print Size 60

Change the Image Resolution 62

Change the Image Canvas Size 64

Revert an Image 66

Duplicate an Image 67

chapter 4 Selection Techniques

Select an Area with a Marquee 70

Select an Area with a Lasso 72

Select an Area with the Magic Wand 76

Select with the Selection Brush 78

Add to or Subtract from a Selection 80

Invert a Selection 82

Grow a Selection 83

Save and Load a Selection 84

TABLE OF CONTENTS

chapter 5 **Manipulating Selections**

Move a Selection 88

Copy and Paste a Selection 90

Delete a Selection 91

Rotate a Selection 92

Scale a Selection 93

Skew or Distort a Selection 94

Feather the Border of a Selection 96

chapter 6 **Layer Basics**

Understanding Layers 100

Add Layers 102

Select a Layer 104

Hide a Layer 105

Move a Layer 106

Duplicate a Layer 107

Change Layer Stacking Order 108

Delete a Layer 110

Create a Layer from a Background 111

Change the Opacity of a Layer 112

Link Layers 113

Merge and Flatten Layers 114

Create a Fill Layer 116

Create an Adjustment Layer 118

Blend Layers 120

Fast Retouching Techniques

Quick Fix a Photo 124

Remove Red Eye 126

Retouch with the Clone Stamp Tool 128

Correct a Spot 130

Remove Dust and Scratches 132

Crop an Image 134

Crop with the Cookie Cutter Tool 136

Rotate an Image 138

Straighten an Image 139

Sharpen an Image 140

chapter 8

Enhancing Contrast and Exposure

Adjust Levels 144

Adjust Shadows and Highlights 146

Change Brightness and Contrast 148

Lighten Areas with the Dodge Tool 150

Darken Areas with the Burn Tool 152

Add a Spotlight 154

Fix an Underexposed Image 156

Using the Blur and Sharpen Tools 158

Enhancing Colors

Adjust Hue and Saturation 162

Adjust Color with the Sponge Tool 164

Correct Color with Color Variations 166

TABLE OF CONTENTS

Replace a Color 168

Equalize Colors 170

Posterize Colors 171

Boost Colors with the Multiply Blending Mode 172

Turn a Color Photo into Black and White 174

Add Color to a Black and White Photo 176

chapter 10 — Painting and Drawing on Photos

Set the Foreground and Background Colors 180

Add Color with the Brush Tool 182

Change Brush Styles 184

Add Color with the Paint Bucket Tool 186

Draw a Shape 188

Draw a Line 190

Erase an Area 192

Apply a Gradient 194

chapter 11 — Applying Filters

Blur an Image 198

Distort an Image 200

Turn an Image into a Painting 202

Turn an Image into a Sketch 204

Add Noise to an Image 206

Pixelate a Photo 208

Emboss an Image 210

chapter 12 Adding Text Elements

Add Text 214
Change the Formatting of Text 216
Change the Color of Text 218
Apply a Filter to Text 220
Create Warped Text 222
Create Outlined Text 224
Add a Drop Shadow to Text 225

chapter 13 Applying Styles and Effects

Add a Drop Shadow to a Photo 228
Add a Drop Shadow to a Layer 230
Frame an Image 232
Add a Fancy Background 234
Add Beveling to a Layer 236
Add an Outer Glow to a Layer 238
Add a Fancy Covering to a Layer 240

TABLE OF CONTENTS

chapter 14

Automating Your Work

Convert File Types 244
Convert Image Sizes 246
Add Watermarks 248
Print a Contact Sheet 250
Print a Picture Package 252

chapter 15

Organize Photos with Organizer

Introducing Organizer 256
Open Organizer 258
Navigate the Organizer Workspace 260
Catalog Photos Stored on Your Computer 262
Catalog Photos from Your Camera 264
Create a New Catalog 266
Open a Catalog 268
View Photos in the Photo Browser 270
View Photos by Date 272
Review Photos as a Slide Show 274
Edit a Photo 276
Delete a Photo 277
Work with Tags 278
Group Photos into a Collection 282
View Photo Properties 284
Add a Caption 286
Find a Photo 288
Backup Photos 290
Create a Slide Show Creation 292

Outputting Files

Add Caption and Copyright Information 298

Save a JPEG for the Web 300

Save a GIF for the Web 302

Preview an Image in a Browser 304

Create a Web Photo Gallery on a PC 306

Create a Postcard on a PC 310

Send an Image with E-mail on a PC 314

Preview a Printout 316

Print an Image from a PC 318

Print an Image from a Mac 320

How to use this Teach Yourself Visually Book

Do you look at the pictures in a book or newspaper before anything else on a page? Would you rather see an image instead of read about how to do something? Search no further. This book is for you. Opening *Teach Yourself VISUALLY Photoshop Elements 3* allows you to read less and learn more about using Photoshop Elements.

Who Needs This Book

This book is highly recommended for the visual learner who wants to learn the basics of Photoshop Elements 3, and who may or may not have prior experience with a computer.

Book Organization

Teach Yourself VISUALLY Photoshop Elements 3 has 16 chapters.

Chapter 1 introduces you to the Photoshop Elements program window, plus basic tools and features.

Chapter 2 shows you how to import photographs from your computer, digital camera, or scanner into Photoshop Elements.

Chapter 3 demonstrates the various ways you can view your photos and change the photo size.

Chapter 4 shows you how to select elements in your photos for editing.

Chapter 5 teaches you how to manipulate selected elements as you prepare for edits.

In Chapter 6, you learn how to use layers to help you edit parts of your images, or the whole image.

Chapter 7 introduces you to handy editing techniques you can apply to quickly fix a photo.

Chapter 8 shows you how to fine-tune tone and contrast problems in your photos.

Chapter 9 teaches you how to adjust colors in a photo.

Chapter 10 introduces you to several tools you can use to draw and paint on your photos.

In Chapter 11, you learn how to apply filters to alter the style and appearance of your photos.

Chapter 12 shows you how to use text tools to add stylized labels and captions to your photos.

Chapter 13 introduces special effects and styles that enable you to transform your photos in interesting ways.

In Chapter 14, you learn how to use the automated features of Elements. This includes resizing collections of images and adding watermarks.

Chapter 15 introduces you to Organizer, a program that works with Photoshop Elements to help you keep track of your many digital image files.

Outputting your photos is covered in Chapter 16. Here, you find out how to create postcards and Web photo galleries, as well as print photos on your printer.

Chapter Organization

This book consists of sections, all listed in the book's table of contents. A *section* is a set of steps that show you how to complete a specific computer task.

Each section, usually contained on two facing pages, has an introduction to the task at hand, a set of full-color screen shots and steps that walk you through the task, and a set of tips. This format allows you to quickly look at a topic of interest and learn it instantly.

Chapters group together three or more sections with a common theme. A chapter may also contain pages that give you the background information needed to understand the sections in a chapter.

What You Need to Use This Book

To perform the tasks in this book, you need a computer installed with one of the following:

Mac Requirements
Apple Mac OS X
128 MB of RAM installed

Windows Requirements
Intel® Pentium® III 800 MHz
Microsoft® Windows® 2000/XP Home/XP Pro256 MB of RAM installed

Using the Mouse

This book uses the following conventions to describe the actions you perform when using the mouse:

Click

Press your left mouse button once. You generally click your mouse on something to select something on the screen.

Double-click

Press your left mouse button twice. Double-clicking something on the computer screen generally opens whatever item you have double-clicked.

Right-click

Press your right mouse button. When you right-click anything on the computer screen, the program displays a shortcut menu containing commands specific to the selected item.

Click and Drag, and Release the Mouse

Move your mouse pointer and hover it over an item on the screen. Press and hold down the left mouse button. Now, move the mouse to where you want to place the item and then release the button. You use this method to move an item from one area of the computer screen to another.

The Conventions in This Book

A number of typographic and layout styles have been used throughout *Teach Yourself VISUALLY Photoshop Elements 3* to distinguish different types of information.

Bold

Bold type represents the names of commands and options that you interact with. Bold type also indicates text and numbers that you must type into a dialog box or window.

Italics

Italic words introduce a new term and are followed by a definition.

Numbered Steps

You must perform the instructions in numbered steps in order to successfully complete a section and achieve the final results.

Bulleted Steps

These steps point out various optional features. You do not have to perform these steps; they simply give additional information about a feature.

Indented Text

Indented text tells you what the program does in response to you following a numbered step. For example, if you click a certain menu command, a dialog box may appear, or a window may open. Indented text may also tell you what the final result is when you follow a set of numbered steps.

Notes

Notes give additional information. They may describe special conditions that may occur during an operation. They may warn you of a situation that you want to avoid, for example the loss of data. A note may also cross reference a related area of the book. A cross reference may guide you to another chapter, or another section with the current chapter.

Icons and buttons

Icons and buttons are graphical representations within the text. They show you exactly what you need to click to perform a step.

You can easily identify the tips in any section by looking for the TIPS icon. Tips offer additional information, including tips, hints, and tricks. You can use the TIPS information to go beyond what you have learn learned in the steps.

Operating System Difference

This book assumes that you are using either Microsoft® Windows® 2000/XP or Mac OS X. Whenever there are difference between these two platforms, the Windows convention is stated first, followed by the Mac convention in parentheses. For example:

3 Press the hold **Alt** (**option** on the Mac) and click the area of the image from which you want to copy.

● You can also right-click (**Control**-click on a Mac) over the image in the Photo Bin and then click Show Filenames.

If you are using an operating system other than Microsoft® Windows® 2000/XP or Mac OS X, — for example, Windows 1997, or Mac OS 9 — there may be significant differences in the screens you see in this book. In addition, the steps presented in this book may significantly differ from your operating system.

Getting Started

Are you interested in working with digital images on your computer? This chapter introduces you to Adobe Photoshop Elements 3, a popular software application for editing and creating digital images.

Introducing Photoshop Elements 3.................4

Understanding Digital Images 6

Start Photoshop Elements on a PC...................8

The Photoshop Elements PC Workspace 9

Start Photoshop Elements on a Mac 10

The Photoshop Elements Mac Workspace 11

Anatomy of the Elements Toolbox 12

Work with Toolbox Tools 14

Work with Palettes 16

Set Program Preferences 20

Find Help 22

Introducing Photoshop Elements 3

Photoshop Elements is a popular photo-editing program you can use to manipulate, modify, and optimize digital images. You can use the program's tools to clean up imperfect snapshots to make them clearer and more colorful, as well as retouch and restore older photos. You can then save the images to print out or use online.

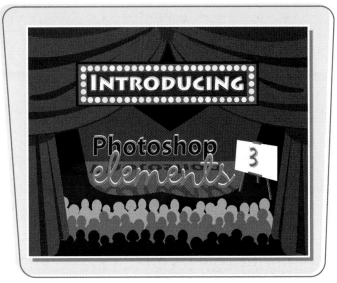

Manipulate Photos

As its name suggests, Photoshop Elements excels at editing elements in your digital photographs. The program includes numerous image-editing tools and palettes of commands you can apply to manipulate the look of your photos. Whether you import photos from a scanner or a digital camera, you can employ a wide variety of editing techniques to your images, from subtle adjustments in color to elaborate filters to make your snapshots look like paintings. See Chapter 5 for more on manipulating selections of your photos. See Chapter 10 to paint and draw on your photos and see Chapter 11 to add filters.

Retouch and Repair

You can use Photoshop Elements to edit new photos as well as retouch and repair older photos that suffer from aging problems. For example, you can restore a faded photo to make it more vibrant, or you can use the Clone Stamp tool to repair a tear or stain. You can also use the program's tools to fix exposure and lighting problems as well as edit out unwanted objects. See Chapter 7 for more on retouching your photos.

Add Elements

Photoshop Elements' painting tools make it a formidable illustration tool as well as a photo editor. You can apply colors or patterns to your images with a variety of brush styles. See Chapter 10 to discover how to paint and draw on your photos. In addition, you can use the application's typographic tools to integrate stylized letters and words into your images. See Chapter 12 for more about adding text elements.

Create a Digital Collage

You can combine different image elements in Photoshop Elements to create new images, or collages. Your compositions can include photos, scanned art, text, and anything else you can save on your computer as a digital image. By placing elements onto separate layers, you can move, transform, and customize them independently of one another. See Chapter 6 for more about layers.

Organize and Catalog

Photoshop Elements offers useful ways to keep your images organized after you edit them. For example, Windows users can place images into catalogs using the new Organizer, a separate component that works with Elements to help you manage libraries of photos. See Chapter 15 to read more about this feature. You can also archive your images on contact sheets. See Chapter 14 for more information.

Put Your Images to Work

After you edit your photographs, you can utilize your images in a variety of ways. Photoshop Elements lets you print your images, save them in a format suitable for placement on a Web page, or prepare them for use in a page-layout program. You can even send your images to someone else with the Attach to E-mail feature. For more on outputting your photos, see Chapter 16.

Understanding Digital Images

To work with photos in Photoshop Elements, you must first turn them into digital format. If you are new to working with digital images, this section introduces you to some important basics.

Acquiring Photos

You can acquire photographic images to use in Photoshop Elements from a number of sources. You can scan in photographs, slides, or artwork and import the images directly into Photoshop Elements. You can also download images from a digital camera. In addition, you can acquire still images, or *frames*, from digital video. For more on importing photos, see Chapter 2.

Understanding Pixels

Digital images in Photoshop Elements consist of tiny, solid-color squares called *pixels*. Photoshop Elements works its magic by rearranging and recoloring these squares. You can edit specific pixels or groups of pixels by selecting the area of the photo you want to edit. If you zoom in close, you can see the pixels that make up your image.

Types of Digital Images

You can use two types of image files in Photoshop Elements: *raster* and *vector*. Most photos you import into Photoshop Elements are raster images. However, when you draw shapes and lines using the Elements tools, you create vector objects. Any text you type into a snapshot is also treated as a vector object.

Vector Images

Vector images use mathematical equations, or vectors, to define an image's shape, color, position, and size. Using equations instead of pixels make the image file size the same regardless of whether the image is large or small. Vector images are easily scaled, unlike bitmap images. Because of their smaller file size, vector images download much more quickly over the Internet.

Bitmap Images

Raster images, also called *bitmap* images, are made up of square dots, called *pixels*. The dots are arranged in a grid pattern, and each dot includes information about its color and position. Most bitmap images use thousands of pixels. As a result, bitmap graphics consume larger file sizes and take longer to download over the Internet.

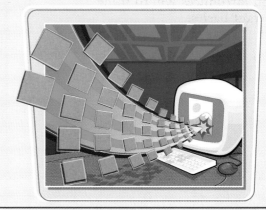

Supported File Formats

Photoshop Elements supports a variety of file types you can both import and export. Popular file formats include BMP, PICT, TIFF, EPS, JPEG, GIF, PNG, and PSD, which stands for Photoshop Document. Files that you save in the PSD format can also be shared with other Adobe programs, such as Photoshop and Illustrator. If you plan to use your images on the Internet, JPEG, GIF, and PNG are the most common formats. PSD format is also quite popular with MacOS X programs.

You can start Photoshop Elements on a PC and begin creating and editing digital images.

① Click **Start**.

② Click **All Programs**.

③ Click **Adobe Photoshop Elements 3**.

Note: *Your path to the Photoshop Elements application may differ depending on how you installed your software.*

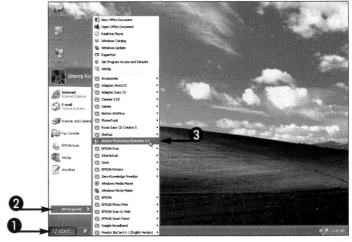

The Photoshop Elements Welcome window opens.

The Welcome window displays clickable shortcuts to common Elements tasks.

④ Click **Edit and Enhance Photos**.

The Photoshop Elements program window opens.

● To change how Elements starts, you can click the Start Up In ☑ to choose an option.

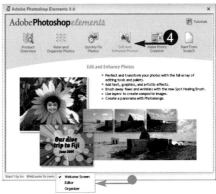

You can use a combination of tools, menu commands, and palette-based features to open and edit your digital images in Photoshop Elements. Learning how to recognize the on-screen elements now can help you use the features later as you edit your digital images.

Shortcuts Bar
Displays clickable icons for common commands.

Edit Mode Tabs
Use these tabs to switch between Quick Fix and Standard Edit modes.

Image Window Controls
Use to tile, minimize, or close the image windows.

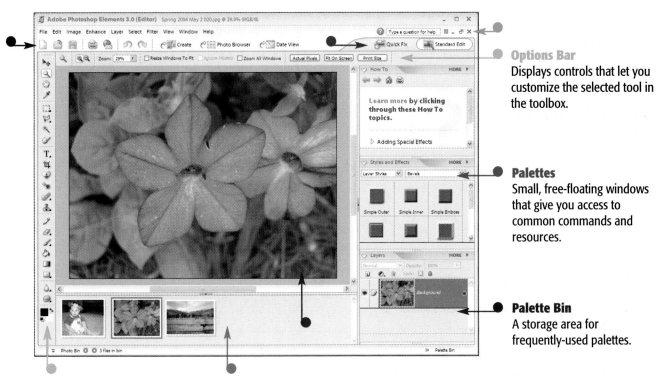

Options Bar
Displays controls that let you customize the selected tool in the toolbox.

Palettes
Small, free-floating windows that give you access to common commands and resources.

Palette Bin
A storage area for frequently-used palettes.

Toolbox
Displays a variety of icons, each one representing an image-editing tool.

Photo Bin
Enables you to open and work with multiple images.

Image Window
Displays each image you open in Photoshop Elements.

Start Photoshop Elements on a Mac

You can start Photoshop Elements on a Macintosh and begin creating and editing digital images.

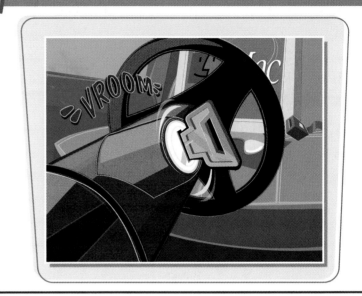

1. Click the Finder icon (🖼) in the Dock.

2. Click the Applications icon (🅰) in the Finder window's sidebar.

3. Double-click the Adobe Photoshop Elements 3 folder icon (📁).

4. Double-click the Photoshop Elements 3 icon (🖼).

Note: The exact location of the Adobe Photoshop Elements icon may be different, depending on how you installed your software and what Mac OS version you have.

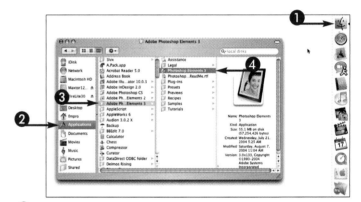

Photoshop Elements starts.

A window appears with clickable shortcuts to common Elements tasks.

● You can click **Close** to close the window.

● You can click the **Show at Startup** option (☑ changes to ☐) to avoid the window in the future.

● To exit the program, click **Photoshop Elements**, **Quit Photoshop Elements**.

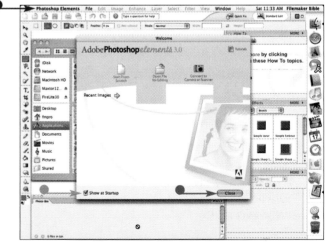

You can use a combination of tools, menu commands, and palette-based features to open and edit your digital images in Photoshop Elements. Learning how to recognize the on-screen elements now can help you use the features later as you edit your digital images.

Shortcuts Bar
Displays clickable icons for common commands.

Image Window Controls
Use to tile, minimize, or close the image windows.

Edit Mode Tabs
Use these tabs to switch between Quick Fix and Standard Edit modes.

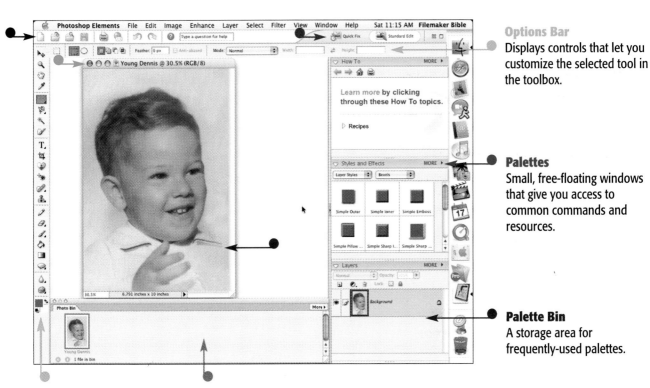

Options Bar
Displays controls that let you customize the selected tool in the toolbox.

Palettes
Small, free-floating windows that give you access to common commands and resources.

Palette Bin
A storage area for frequently-used palettes.

Toolbox
Displays a variety of icons, each one representing an image-editing tool.

Photo Bin
Enables you to open and work with multiple images.

Image Window
Displays each image you open in Photoshop Elements.

To aid in manipulating photos, Photoshop Elements provides a myriad of specialized tools that perform a variety of editing techniques. Take time to familiarize yourself with the toolbox tools.

Move
Moves selected areas.

Zoom
Zooms your view of an image in or out.

Hand
Views unseen parts of larger images.

Eyedropper
Samples color of an area in an image.

Marquee
Selects pixels by drawing a box or ellipse around the area to edit.

Lasso
Selects pixels by drawing a free-form shape around the area to edit.

Magic Wand
Selects pixels of odd-shaped areas based on similar pixel color.

Selection Brush
Selects pixels using brush shapes.

Type
Adds type to an image.

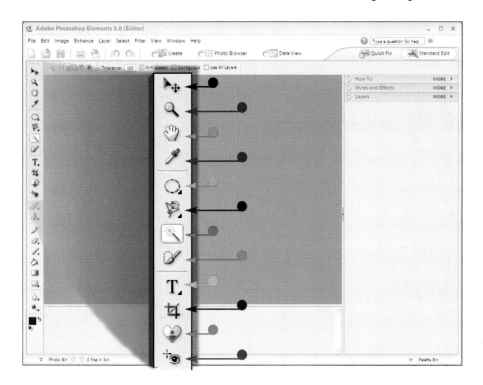

Red-Eye Removal
Corrects red-eye problems.

Cookie Cutter
Crops your image to shapes.

Crop
Trims an image to create a new size.

Spot Healing Brush
Quickly fixes slight imperfections by cloning nearby pixels.

Clone Stamp
Duplicates an area of the image.

Pencil
Draws freehand lines or strokes.

Eraser
Erases pixels.

Brush
Paints brush strokes.

Paint Bucket
Fills areas with color.

Gradient
Creates blended color effects to use as fills.

Custom Shape
Draws predefined shapes.

Blur
Blurs hard edges.

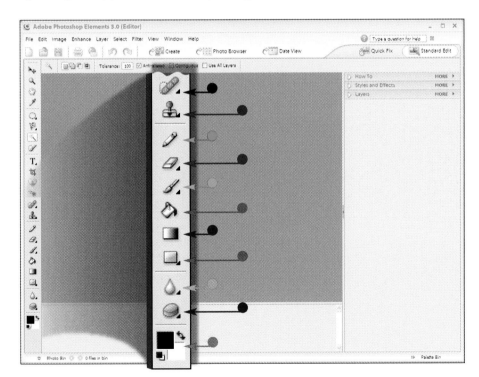

Foreground & Background Color
Sets foreground and background colors.

Sponge
Adjusts color saturation or intensity.

Work with Toolbox Tools

You can use the toolbox tools to make changes to an image. You can move the mouse pointer over a tool to display the tool name. After you click a tool, the Options bar displays controls for customizing how the tool works. Some tools include a tiny triangle in the corner indicating hidden tools you can select. For example, the Marquee tool includes two variations of marquees: Rectangular and Elliptical.

SELECT A TOOL

① Click a tool.

● The Options bar displays customizing options for the selected tool.

② Click any options you want to set for the tool.

SELECT A HIDDEN TOOL

① Click a tool.

② Hold down the mouse button.

A menu of hidden tools appears.

③ Click the tool you want to use.

Elements displays the last tool you selected in a group of hidden tools.

MOVE THE TOOLBOX

1️⃣ Position the ⌖ over the top of the docked toolbox.

2️⃣ Drag the toolbox to a new location on the screen.

3️⃣ Release the mouse button.

● Photoshop Elements displays the toolbox as a floating palette.

You can drag the toolbox to another location by dragging the top of the palette.

TIPS

Can I close the floating toolbox?

Yes. Closing the toolbox palette closes the toolbox entirely so that the tools no longer appear on-screen. To close the floating toolbox palette, click **Window**, and then click **Tools**. To open the palette again, click **Window**, and then **Tools** again.

How do I dock my floating toolbox again?

Move the ⌖ over the top of the toolbox palette, and then drag the toolbox to the left side of the program window. Photoshop Elements automatically docks it for you when you drag close enough to the left edge of the window.

Work with Palettes

You can open free-floating windows called *palettes* to access different Photoshop Elements commands and features. You can store the palettes you use the most in the Palette Bin for quick access when you need them. You can collapse and expand palettes in the Palette Bin.

For more on the location of the Palette Bin, see the section "The Photoshop Elements PC Workspace."

Work with Palettes

EXPAND OR COLLAPSE A PALETTE IN THE PALETTE BIN

1 Click the arrow next to the palette name in the Palette Bin.

● Click the Expand arrow (▷) to display a collapsed palette.

● Click the Collapse arrow (▽) to collapse a palette from view.

● In this example, the Layers palette now displays.

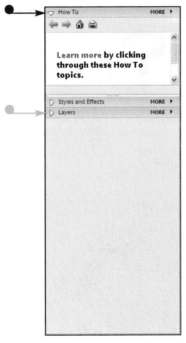

OPEN A NEW PALETTE

1 Click **Window**.

2 Click the palette name.

A check mark (☑) next to the palette name indicates the palette is already open.

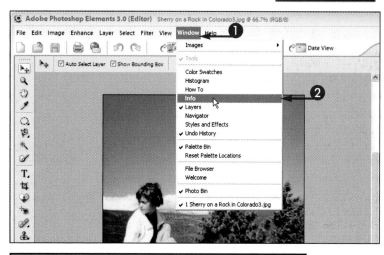

● The palette opens.

You can move the palette by dragging its title bar.

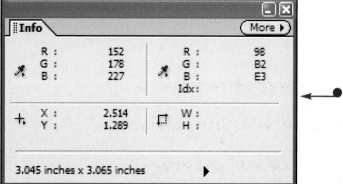

 TIPS

How do I add a palette to the palette bin?

Open the palette as a free-floating window and then click the palette menu's **More** button. This displays a menu of related palette commands. Next, click **Place in Palette Bin**. After you close the palette, Photoshop Elements adds the palette to the Palette Bin.

How do I minimize a free-floating palette?

Double-click the palette's title to minimize the palette window. To view the full palette again, double-click the title. You can also click the tiny Minimize (▬, ⊟ on a Mac) and Maximize (▢, ⊡ on a Mac) buttons on the palette window to control the palette's display.

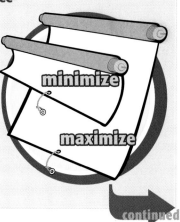

continued

You can move palettes around
the program window to suit the
way you work. You can close a
palette you no longer want to
view. You can also hide the
Palette Bin to free up more on-
screen workspace.

Work with Palettes *(continued)*

MOVE A PALETTE

① Click and drag the palette title to the work area.

② Release the mouse.

The palette opens as a free-floating window.

● You can click the **More** button to access
commands relevant to the palette.

You can resize the Palette Bin by dragging the
bin's border.

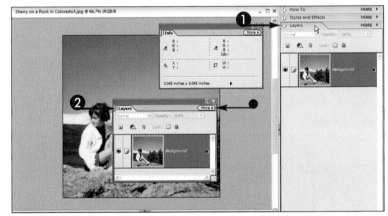

CLOSE A PALETTE

① Click the Close button ⊠ (▣).

The palette closes.

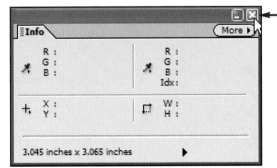

CLOSE THE PALETTE BIN

1 Click the Close Palette Bin button (⬚).

You can also click **Window** and then click **Palette Bin**.

Mac users can open and close the bin through the **Window** menu.

The Palette Bin closes.

● To display the bin again, click the Open Palette Bin button (⬚).

TIP

Can I customize a palette?

You can customize some of the palettes in Photoshop Elements. For example, you can change the size of the thumbnail image that appears in the Layers palette. To customize a palette, follow these steps.

1 Click **More**.

2 Click **Palette Options**.

The palette's Options dialog box opens.

3 Make any changes to the palette options.

4 Click **OK**.

Elements applies the changes to the palette.

Set Program Preferences

Photoshop Elements' Preferences dialog box lets you change default settings and customize how the program looks. The Preferences dialog box includes ten categories: General, Saving Files, Display & Cursors, Transparency, Units & Rulers, Grid, Plug-Ins & Scratch Disks, Memory & Image Cache, and File Browser. Windows users see an extra set of preferences, Organize & Share, for setting up organizing options. You can view and select from different settings in each category.

Set Program Preferences

① Click **Edit** (**Photoshop Elements** on a Mac).

② Click **Preferences**.

③ Click **General**.

The Preferences dialog box appears and displays General options.

④ Select any settings you want to change.

Note: Each category in the Preferences dialog box reveals a different set of customizing options.

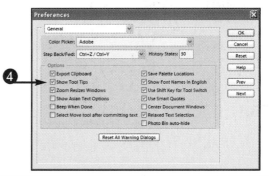

- Click here for a list of other category settings you can select and view in the Preferences dialog box.

- You can also click **Prev** and **Next** to move back and forth between categories.

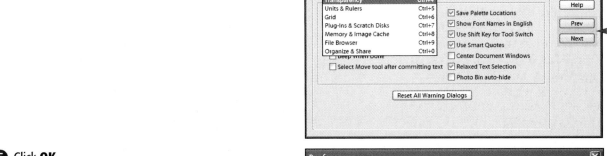

5 Click **OK**.

Photoshop Elements sets preferences to your specifications.

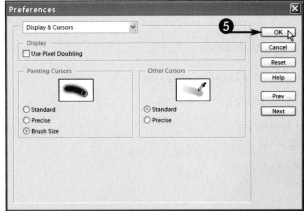

TIPS

What type of measurement units should I use in Elements?

Typically, you should use the units most applicable to the type of output you intend to use. Pixel units are useful for Web imaging because monitor dimensions are measured in pixels. Inches or picas are useful for print because those are standards for working on paper. You can find measurement settings in the Units & Rulers preferences.

How do I allocate extra memory to Elements for opening more image files?

Digital image-editing programs can use up a lot of memory on your computer, called random access memory (RAM). The Memory & Image Cache preferences show how much memory you have available and how much of it Photoshop Elements will use. You can make changes to these settings to enhance the program's performance. The Plug-Ins & Scratch Disks preferences enable you to allocate extra memory on your hard drive, called *scratch disk space*, to use if your computer runs out of RAM. You can specify up to four different hard drives, including removable flash memory or partitions, if you have more than one.

Photoshop Elements comes with plenty of electronic documentation that you can access in case you ever need help.

❶ Click **Help**.

❷ Click **Photoshop Elements Help**.

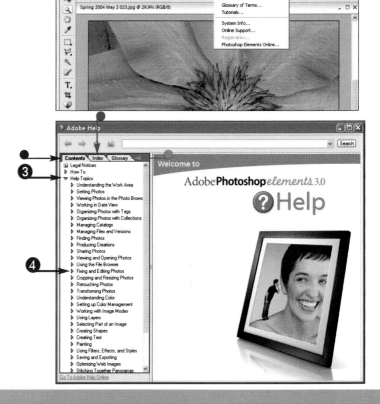

The Adobe Help window opens.

● The Contents tab displays a list of topics you can consult for additional help.

● The Index tab lists the help topics alphabetically.

● The Glossary tab lists terms associated with Photoshop Elements.

❸ Click the Help Topics ▷ to display a list of help topics.

❹ Click ▷ to view a list of subtopics.

⑤ Click the topic you want to view.

The Help window displays information about the topic in the right frame.

● You can scroll through the information and click links to learn more about a topic.

● You can click this link to visit the Adobe Web site for more help.

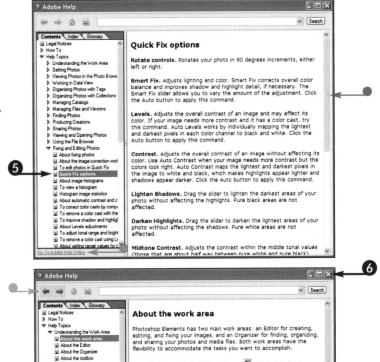

● You can click the Go Back (◄) and Go Forward (►) buttons to move between topics.

⑥ Click ⊠ (🖫).

The Adobe Help window closes.

TIPS

How do I search for a particular topic?

You can use the Search text box at the top of the Help window to look up keywords in the Help files. Simply click in the text box and type in your keyword or words and then click **Search**. Photoshop Elements displays any matching search results. You can also type keywords in the Search text box at the top of the program window to look up help information.

How can I get additional tips and news about Photoshop Elements?

Click **Help** and then click **Online Support** to open your Web browser and display the Photoshop Elements Web page. Here you can access information about product support, software upgrades, and third-party add-ons for Photoshop Elements. You need an Internet connection to get information via Adobe Online.

CHAPTER 2

Acquiring and Storing Digital Images

Before you can start working with photos in Photoshop Elements, you must first turn your photos into digital form. This chapter shows you how to import images and perform basic file tasks.

Find Images for Your Projects 26

Import Images from a Scanner 28

Import Images from a Digital Camera 30

Import Images from a Card Reader 32

Import Images Using Organizer on a PC 34

Download Images with Adobe Photo
    Downloader 38

Import Images from a Video 42

Save an Image 44

Close an Image 45

Open an Image 46

Create a New Image 48

Find Images for Your Projects

In order to work with images in Photoshop Elements, you must first acquire the images. You can get raw material for Elements from a variety of sources.

Digital Photos

Digital cameras are a great way to get digital images onto your computer. Most digital cameras save their images in JPEG or TIFF format, both of which you can open and edit in Photoshop Elements. You can transfer images directly from a camera using a USB cable, or you can transfer images using a card reader, a device that reads your camera's memory card.

Scanned Photos and Art

A scanner gives you an inexpensive way to convert existing paper-based content into digital form. You can scan photos and art into your computer, retouch and stylize them in Photoshop Elements, and then output them to a color printer.

Clip Art

If you want a wide variety of image content to work with, consider buying a clip art collection. Such collections usually include illustrations, photos, and decorative icons that you can use in imaging projects. Most software stores sell clip art; you can also buy downloadable clip art online.

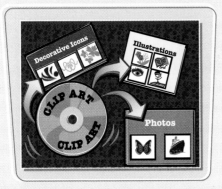

Web Images

If you have photos or art stored on the Web, you can easily save those image files to your computer and then open them up in Photoshop Elements. In Microsoft Internet Explorer on the PC, you can save a Web image by right-clicking it and selecting the **Save Picture As** command. In Safari on the Mac, you can Control-click an image and select **Save Image As** in the menu that appears.

Start from Scratch

You can also create your Photoshop Elements image from scratch by opening a blank canvas in the image window. Then you can apply color and patterns with Photoshop's painting tools or cut and paste parts of other images to create a composite. See the section "Create a New Image" for more on opening a blank canvas.

Sample Images

Photoshop Elements comes with several example images that you can open and experiment with. They are useful if you have nothing else to work with and want to get started right away. You can find the images inside the Elements application folder in a subfolder called Samples.

Import Images from a Scanner

You can bring photos into Photoshop Elements through a scanning device attached to your computer. You can scan black and white and color photos to import into Elements. To scan an image, make sure the scanner is hooked up properly before you begin.

Every scanner works differently, so be sure to consult the documentation that came with your scanner for more information.

Import Images from a Scanner

① Click **File**.

② Click **Import**.

③ Click the name of your scanner device.

The device's scan manager or associated software launches.

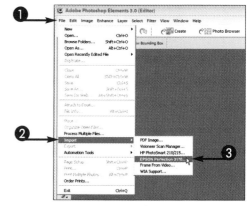

④ Using the scan manager or software associated with your scanner, change any settings as needed.

For example, you may need to specify if the photo is black and white or color.

Note: Because scanner software varies by manufacturers, be sure to consult the documentation that came with your device.

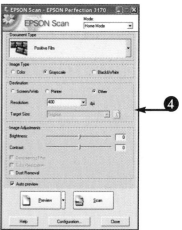

⑤ Click **Scan**.

The image is scanned and added to the Elements workspace.

⑥ Click **Close** or **Exit** to close the software.

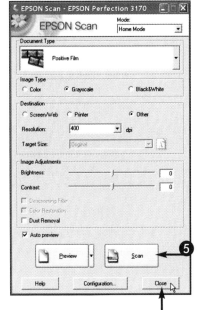

You can now edit the photo as needed.

Photoshop Elements does not recognize my scanner. What can I do?

If the Import menu does not list your scanner, and you know it is hooked up and working properly, consider using your scanning software to scan the images instead. Then you can open them as files in Photoshop Elements using the Open dialog box. See the section "Open an Image" for more about using this dialog box.

Can I scan in artwork or documents to use with my photos?

Yes. You can scan in paper-based artwork and other documents and use them with your photos. You can create collages and place the scanned files in separate layers in Photoshop Elements. For example, you can scan in a small drawing and superimpose it over a photograph. For more on working with layers, see Chapter 6.

Import Images from a Digital Camera

You can bring photos into Photoshop Elements through a digital camera attached to your computer. Many digital cameras manufactured today connect to a computer using a USB cable and a USB port. For PCs, you typically find this port on the back of the computer. For Macs, you may find the port on the side or front of the CPU, on the side of the monitor, or on the keyboard. Make sure the camera is hooked up properly before you begin.

Every camera works differently, so be sure to consult the documentation that came with your digital camera for more information. The steps in this section work with Windows XP and OS X. If you use a card reader to transfer images rather than a USB cable, see the section "Import Images from a Card Reader" for more information.

Import Images from a Digital Camera

① Click **File**.

② Click **Import**.

③ Click the name of your digital camera.

   The associated software for the camera launches.

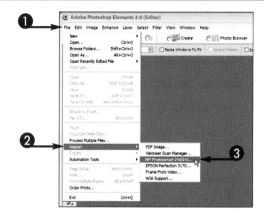

④ Using the software associated with your camera, click the image you want to import.

● You may need to scroll through the images to find the one you want.

● You can also import more than one photo.

   Many cameras allow you to import all the photos from the memory card at once.

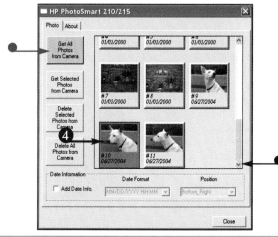

⑤ Click the button for acquiring the image.

In this example, the Get Selected Photos from Camera button is clicked.

The image appears in the Photoshop Elements workspace.

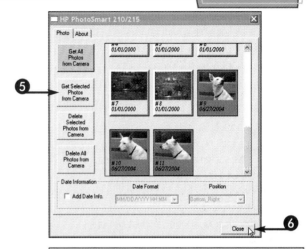

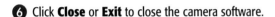

⑥ Click **Close** or **Exit** to close the camera software.

The newly imported images appear in Photoshop Elements ready for edits.

My camera is not listed in the Import menu. Why not?

Windows XP

Make sure you installed the camera's software properly, including any necessary driver files for communicating with your computer and other programs. You must also connect the device to your computer and make sure you properly activate the device in order to import photos. If you still have trouble, try importing the images through the File Browser or the Organizer window. See the section "Import Images Using Organizer on a PC" for more information.

Mac OS X

Because of OS X's great built-in support for USB cameras, digital camera vendors generally do not provide OS X driver files. Therefore, your cameras do not appear in the Import menu. To import photos, use either the Image Capture or iPhoto software that comes with your Mac. After you import a photo onto your computer, you can use Elements to do any editing or touchup work.

Import Images from a Card Reader

You can use Photoshop Element's File Browser feature to import images from other drives and folders, including a digital card reader. Many digital cameras today store images on a digital card, a small storage device you can remove from the camera and insert into a card reader attached to the computer. Your computer treats a card reader as a separate drive.

Make sure that you attach the card reader properly, and the memory card is completely inserted before importing images. Consult the documentation that came with your digital camera and card reader for more information.

Import Images from a Card Reader

1 Click **Window**.

2 Click **File Browser**.

The File Browser window opens.

You can also click **File** and then click **Browse Folders** to open the File Browser window.

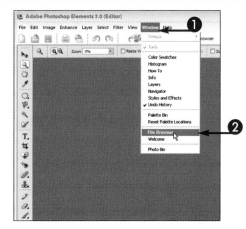

3 Navigate to the card reader drive.

You can click the Expand (▷, ► on a Mac) or Collapse (▽, ▼ on a Mac) icons to display and hide drives and folders.

Note: You can also use the File Browser to open other image files stored on your computer.

4 Open the folder containing the digital camera's images.

● The File Browser window displays the images stored on the card.

5 Click the photo or photos you want to import.

To select multiple images, press **Ctrl** (**⌘** on a Mac) while clicking each image.

6 Click **File**.

7 Click **Open**.

The newly imported images appear in Photoshop Elements.

The File Browser remains open in the background.

8 Click **Window**.

9 Click **File Browser**.

The File Browser feature closes.

TIP

I cannot see the File Browser. How do I view the window when it is hidden or only partially visible?

If you know the File Browser window is open, yet cannot see it fully on-screen, you can hide the Photo Bin and the Palette Bin to free up viewing room in the workspace area. Click the Close Photo Bin button (⬇) and click the Close Palette Bin button (▷). Mac users can click **Windows** and then click **Palette Bin** to close the Palette bin. You may also need to minimize any open image windows. See Chapter 3 for more on working with image windows.

Import Images Using Organizer on a PC

On a PC, you can use Photoshop Element's Organizer program to import images from digital cameras or card readers. Organizer is a separate application that works alongside Photoshop Elements.

You can use Organizer to manage libraries of images. See Chapter 15 for more about this program.

On the Mac, use your iPhoto tools to organize your photos. For more on iPhoto tools, see *Teach Yourself VISUALLY iLife '04.*

① Click **Photo Browser**.

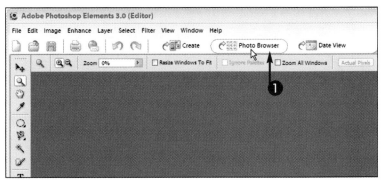

The Organizer program opens.

② Click the Get Photos button ( ).

③ Click **From Camera or Card Reader**.

You can also import images from a scanner, mobile phone, online service, or from your own computer folders.

The Get Photos from Camera or Card Reader dialog box opens.

④ Click here and click your camera or card reader.

The stored images appear here.

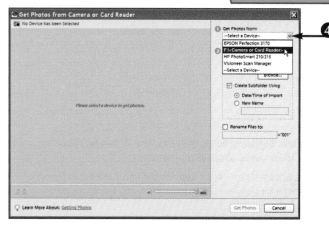

⑤ Click to select or deselect the images you want to import (☑ changes to ☐ or ☐ changes to ☑).

● You can create a folder in which to store the images by clicking the **Create Subfolder Using** (☑ changes to ☐) and **New Name** (○ changes to ◉) options, and then typing a name for the folder.

⑥ Click **Get Photos**.

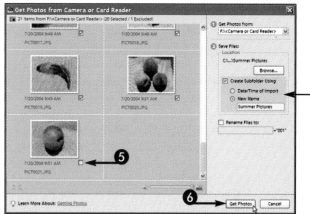

 TIPS

Do I always need to create a new folder for my images?

Organizing new image files when you upload them from a camera or card reader onto your computer is a good idea. The Organizer program can help you keep your digital photos sorted into easy-to-identify folders so you can quickly find the image you want later. If you prefer to store the subfolder in another location, simply click **Browse** in the Get Photos from Camera or Card Reader dialog box and navigate to the main folder where you want to store the files.

How do I change the default image file names?

By default, Organizer names the image files numerically preceded with the name PICT. To change to another naming system for your current imports, click the **Rename Files To** option (☐ changes to ☑) in the Get Photos from Camera or Card Reader dialog box and type a new name for the images, such as VACATION or BIRTHDAY. Organizer automatically adds numbers for each photo for you.

continued

After you import your photos, you can choose which ones you want to edit in Photoshop Elements. To perform any edits, you must return to the Elements editor window. Organizer remains open until you close the program window.

Import Images Using Organizer on a PC *(continued)*

Organizer displays a message box about the imported images.

⑦ Click **OK**.

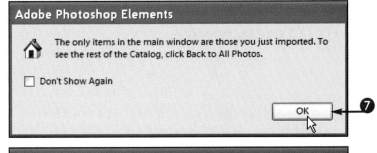

Organizer asks if you want to delete the selected images from the camera or card reader.

⑧ Click **Yes** to delete or **No** to leave the images on the camera or storage card.

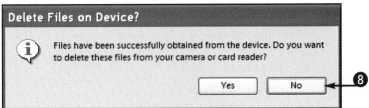

The Organizer window displays the imported images.

9 Click the image you want to edit in Photoshop Elements.

10 Click the **Standard Edit** button.

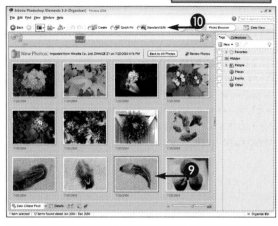

Photoshop Elements displays the image you want to edit.

The Organizer window remains open for you to work with more photos in your library.

You can return to the Organizer window and click ⊠ (▣) to exit the application.

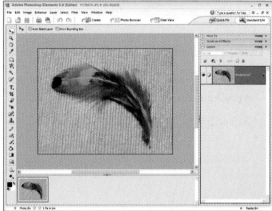

Does Organizer have any photo-editing tools I can apply?

Organizer is primarily an image-management tool you can use to help you keep track of the many photos you store on your computer. You can use the Auto Fix Photo command to make some quick adjustments to a photo. This feature borrows from Photoshop Elements Quick Fix tools, which read an image and make automatic adjustments to problem areas, such as tone and brightness. To apply the Auto Fix feature to any photo in Organizer, right-click the image and click **Auto Fix Photo**. If you do not like the changes, click **Edit** and then click **Undo Auto Fix**. For best editing results, use Photoshop Elements to make changes to your images.

Download Images with Adobe Photo Downloader

On a PC, you can use the Adobe Photo Downloader to download images from your digital camera or card reader and display them in the Organizer program. Adobe Photo Downloader opens automatically when you plug in your camera or card reader to transfer your pictures.

Organizer works alongside Photoshop Elements to help you to manage libraries of images. See Chapter 15 for more about this program.

On the Mac, use your iPhoto tools to organize your photos. For more on iPhoto tools, see *Teach Yourself VISUALLY iLife '04.*

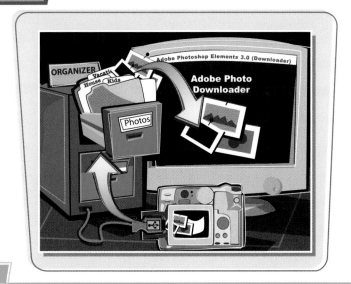

Download Images with Adobe Photo Downloader

① Plug your digital camera or card reader into your computer.

Adobe Photo Downloader opens automatically.

● If your camera or card reader is not already displayed, click here and click the appropriate device.

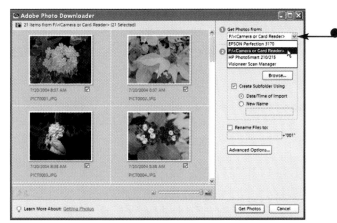

② Click **Browse**.

The Browse For Folder dialog box opens.

③ Navigate to the folder where you want to download and store your images.

● You can click here to start a new folder for the images.

④ Click **OK**.

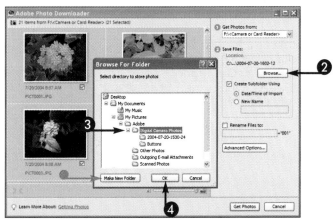

5 Click the **Rename Files to** option (☐ changes to ☑).

6 Type a name for the newly downloaded files.

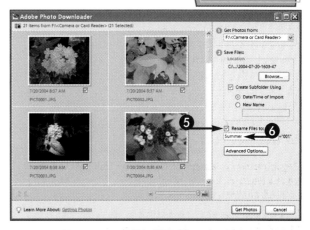

7 Click to select or deselect the images you want to download (☑ changes to ☐ or ☐ changes to ☑).

● You can use the scroll buttons to scroll through the stored images.

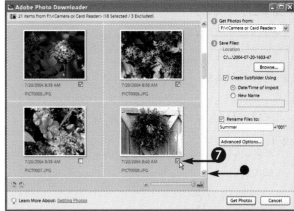

TIPS

I connected my camera to my computer but Adobe Photo Downloader does not start. What do I do?

If Adobe Photo Downloader does not launch immediately, you can use Organizer to import files from your camera or card reader. See the previous section, "Import Images Using Organizer on a PC," for more information. Organizer uses an identical feature, the Get Photos from Camera or Card Reader dialog box, to transfer image files. You can also import images using the File Browser in Photoshop Elements. See the section "Import Images from a Digital Camera" for more on using File Browser.

Do I have to use a Photoshop Elements program to transfer images to my computer?

No. You can use the software that came with your camera or card reader to transfer files to a designated storage area on your computer. Be sure to read the documentation that came with the device to learn more about the steps you need to follow. Once you transfer the images, you can then open the images in Photoshop Elements to perform edits.

continued

You can select exactly which pictures you download from your camera or memory card with Adobe Photo Downloader. You can also specify a naming system for the files to help you locate the photos later. After Adobe Photo Downloader transfers the images, you can choose to delete the files from the camera or digital storage card.

Download Images with Adobe Photo Downloader (continued)

8 Click **Get Photos**.

Adobe Photo Downloader starts downloading the image files from the camera or storage card to Organizer.

A message box appears detailing information about the downloaded images.

9 Click **OK**.

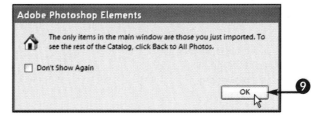

A message prompt asks if you want to delete the selected images from the camera or card reader.

⑩ Click **Yes** to delete or **No** to leave the images on the camera or storage card.

The Organizer window displays the downloaded images.

***Note:** See the section "Import Images Using Organizer on a PC" for more on the Organizer program.*

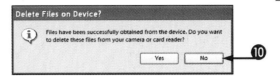

TIP

How do I edit an image I just downloaded?

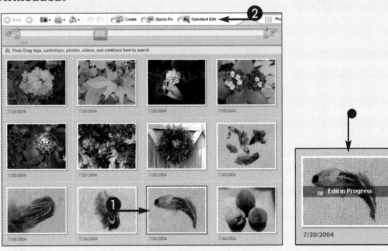

① Select the image in Organizer.

② Click the **Standard Edit** button.

Photoshop Elements displays the image file for editing.

● Organizer displays an Edit in Progress message.

When you finish editing the image, you can save the file and return to Organizer to choose another image to edit.

Import Images from a Video

You can capture frames from a video and import them into Photoshop Elements. You can capture frames from a digital video camcorder hooked up to your computer, or you can capture frames from a video file stored on your hard drive. If capturing directly from a camcorder, make sure the device is hooked up properly before you begin.

Every camcorder works differently, so consult the documentation that came with your device for more information.

Elements supports AVI, ASF, WMV, MPG, MPEG, and QuickTime file formats for Windows, among others. Elements also supports AVI, QuickTime, MPEG, and a number of other formats for Mac. For more on working with file formats, see Chapter 16.

① Click **File**.

② Click **Import**.

③ Click **Frame From Video**.

The Frame From Video dialog box opens.

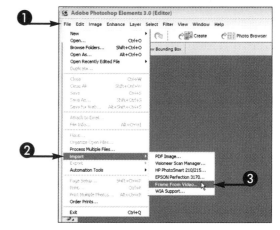

④ Click **Browse**.

The Open dialog box appears.

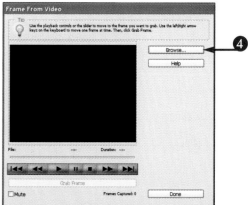

⑤ Click the video file from which you want to import a frame.

● In Windows, you can click here to search a specific folder or drive.

On a Mac, you can scroll through the browser pane to find the folder you want.

⑥ Click **Open**.

You can also double-click the file name to open the file.

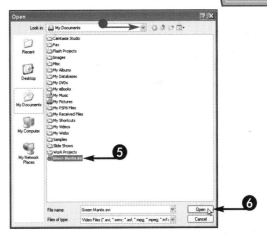

⑦ Click the playback controls to cue the video to the frame you want to import.

⑧ Click **Grab Frame**.

⑨ Click **Done**.

● The newly imported image appears in the Elements workspace ready for edits.

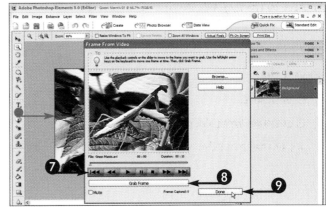

TIP

Can I import PDF files?
Yes. PDF, which stands for Portable Document Format, is a common Adobe format for storing both vector and bitmap information. Photoshop Elements recognizes both generic PDF files created in other applications as well as the PDF format you can create in Elements. You can find an option for importing PDF files on the **Import** submenu.

Save an Image

You can save an image in Photoshop Elements to store any changes that you make to it. PSD is the default file format for Elements. Elements supports a variety of other image file formats, including the popular JPEG, GIF, and PNG formats commonly found on the Internet.

Consider saving your images regularly to avoid losing important changes in the event of a system crash.

Save an Image

1 Click **File**.

2 Click **Save As**.

Note: *For images that you have previously saved, you can click **File** and then **Save**.*

The Save As dialog box appears.

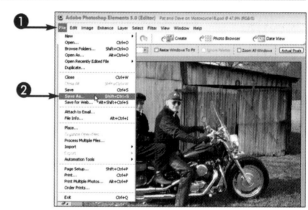

3 Type a name for the file.

● In Windows, you can click here and select another folder or drive to store the file.

On a Mac, you can click in the Where box, use the Sidebar, or use the column or list browsers to select a folder or drive.

● You can click here to select another file format.

4 Click **Save**.

Photoshop Elements saves the image file.

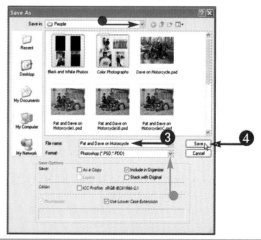

You can close an image file after you finish working on restoring and retouching the image. Closing a file frees up memory, which can conserve the power your computer needs to process files. Although you can certainly have more than one image file open at a time, closing files you no longer need can speed up your computer's performance.

Close an Image

1 Click **File**.

2 Click **Close**.

You can also right-click (Control-click on a Mac) on a photo in the Photo Bin and click **Close**.

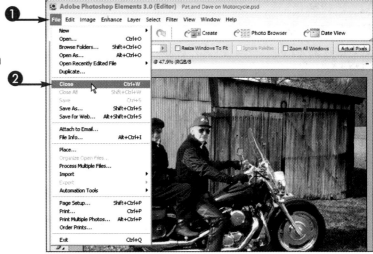

Note: If you have not saved the file, Elements prompts you to do so before closing the file. Click **Yes** to save your work.

On a Mac, OS X indicates unsaved documents with a block dot in the Close button (●).

Note: See the section "Save an Image " for more on how to save files.

Photoshop Elements closes the image file but leaves the program window open.

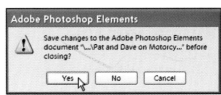

Open an Image

You can open an existing image file in Photoshop Elements to modify it or use it in a project. Existing files are images you previously imported into Elements.

OPEN AN EXISTING IMAGE

① Click **File**.

② Click **Open**.

You can also click the Open button (🖼️) in the Shortcuts bar to open the file.

The Open dialog box appears.

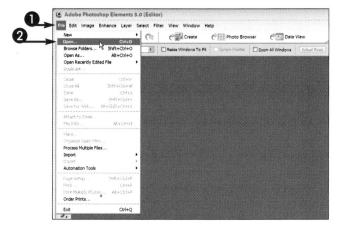

③ Navigate to the folder containing the file you want to open.

● In Windows, you can click here to browse folders.

On a Mac, you can click in the Where box, use the Sidebar, or use the column or list browsers to select a folder or drive.

④ Click the filename.

● A preview of the image displays.

⑤ Click **Open**.

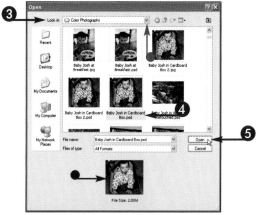

Photoshop Elements opens the image.

● If the Photo Bin is displayed, the image also appears in the bin.

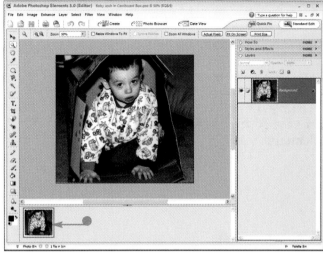

OPEN RECENTLY ACCESSED IMAGES

① Click **File**.

② Click **Open Recently Edited File**.

A list of recently opened files displays.

③ Click the image's filename.

Photoshop Elements opens the image.

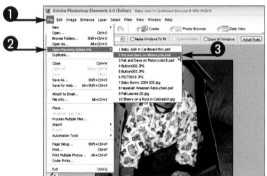

What types of files can Photoshop Elements open?
Photoshop Elements can open most of the image file formats in common use today. Here are a few of the more popular ones:

Format	Description
BMP (Bitmap)	The standard Windows image format
TIFF (Tagged Image File Format)	A popular format for print on Windows and Macintosh
EPS (Encapsulated PostScript)	Another print-oriented format
JPEG (Joint Photographic Experts Group)	A format for Web images
GIF (Graphics Interchange Format)	Another format for Web images
PSD (Photoshop Document)	Photoshop's native file format

Create a
New Image

You can start a Photoshop Elements project by creating a blank image. For example, you can create a collage by adding parts of other images to a newly created image.

① Click **File**.

② Click **New**.

③ Click **Blank File**.

The New dialog box appears.

You can also click the New button ([▢]) on the Shortcuts bar to open the New dialog box.

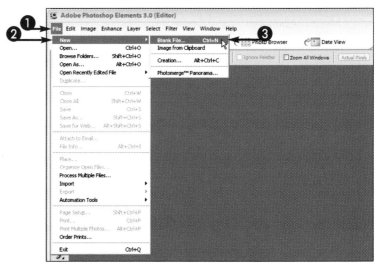

④ Type a name for the new image.

⑤ Type the desired dimensions and resolution or click to select a preset dimension and resolution.

● You can click here to change the background of the blank canvas.

⑥ Click **OK**.

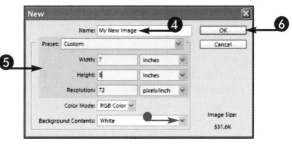

Photoshop Elements creates a new image window at the specified dimensions.

7 Use the Photoshop Elements tools and commands to create your image.

In this example, part of another image was cut and pasted into the window and rotated.

Note: To save your image, see the section "Save an Image."

TIPS

How do I choose a resolution for a new image?

The appropriate resolution depends on how you will eventually use the image. For Web or multimedia images, select 72 pixels/inch — the standard resolution for on-screen images. To print black and white images on regular paper on a laser printer, 150 pixels/inch probably suffices. For full-color magazine or brochure images, you should use a higher resolution — at least 250 pixels/inch.

How do I insert a clip art file into my blank image?

You can use the Place command to add clip art and other original computer artwork to your Photoshop Elements image file. This command only works on file formats associated with artwork saved as vector graphic, which includes AI, EPS, PDF, and PDP formats. To activate the command, click **File**, and then click **Place**. This opens the Place dialog box and you can navigate to the clip art you want to use.

CHAPTER

3

Image Basics

Are you ready to start working with images? This chapter shows you how to fine-tune your workspace. Discover how to change the on-screen image size, set a print size, and change the print resolution.

Work with Image Windows................................52

Magnify with the Zoom Tool.......................54

Adjust the Image View...............................56

Change the Image Size...............................58

Change the Image Print Size 60

Change the Image Resolution 62

Change the Image Canvas Size 64

Revert an Image...66

Duplicate an Image....................................67

Work with Image Windows

Each image you open in Photoshop Elements appears in its own window. You can minimize and maximize image windows and tile multiple image windows in the workspace. If you have more than one image open, you can use the Photo Bin to switch between image windows.

① Open two or more images.

Note: *See Chapter 2 for more on opening image files.*

● The active, or current, image appears here.

● The Photo Bin displays all the open images.

② Click the image you want to view.

   If your open images fill the Photo Bin, you can use the scroll arrows to scroll to the image you want to open.

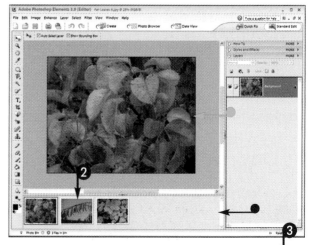

● The image you select appears as the active image.

③ Click the Automatically Tile Windows button (⊞).

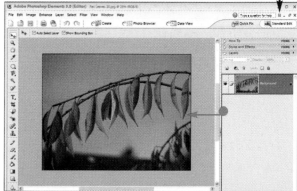

● Photoshop Elements displays all the open image files in individual windows in the workspace.

④ Click the Maximize Mode button (□).

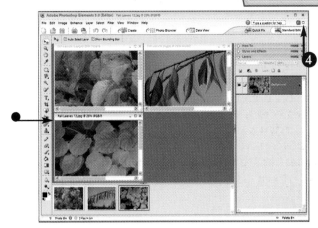

Photoshop Elements displays the active image in the workspace.

⑤ Click ⊠ (⊗ on a Mac).

Elements closes the image window.

You can also right-click (Control -click on the Mac) on an image in the Photo Bin and click **Close** to close an image.

TIPS

Is there a way to close or hide the Photo Bin?

Yes. You can close the Photo Bin and the Palette Bin to free up more workspace on-screen. To close the Photo Bin, click the **Close Photo Bin** icon (▽, ⊗ on a Mac). To close the Palette Bin on a PC, click **Close Palette Bin** (▷).
To close the Palette Bin on a Mac, click **Window** and then click **Palette Bin**. To open either bin, click their respective icons again. You can also open and close the bins through the **Window** menu.

Where else can I find commands for controlling my image windows?

You can click **Window** and then click **Images** to find a submenu of window commands. For example, you can cascade your open images across the workspace or tile them side-by-side. If you are comparing several photos on-screen, you can click **Match Location** to view the same area in each open window. You can click **Match Zoom** to view the same zoom percentage in each open window.

Magnify with the Zoom Tool

You can change the magnification of an image with the Zoom tool. This enables you to view small details in an image or view an image at full size.

INCREASE MAGNIFICATION

1 Click the Zoom tool ( ).

2 Click the image.

Photoshop Elements increases the magnification of the image.

The point that you clicked in the image is centered in the window.

The current magnification shows in the image title bar and Options bar.

● You can select an exact magnification by typing a percentage value or dragging the Zoom slider in the Options bar.

DECREASE MAGNIFICATION

❶ Click the Zoom Out button (🔍).

❷ Click the image.

Photoshop Elements decreases the magnification of the image.

Note: *You can also press and hold* Alt *(* option *on a Mac) and click the image to decrease magnification.*

MAGNIFY A DETAIL

❶ Click the Zoom In button (🔍).

❷ Click and drag with the Zoom tool to select the detail.

The area appears enlarged on-screen.

The more you zoom in, the more pixels you see and the less you see of the image's content.

 TIPS

How do I quickly return an image to 100% magnification?

Double-click 🔍 in the toolbox, click **Actual Pixels** on the Options bar, or click **View** and then **Actual Pixels**. To zoom the image to workspace size, click **Fit On Screen** on the Options bar.

How can I find out the filename of the image I am viewing?

Depending on how you are viewing images in the workspace, individual image windows can show the name of the file, or you can look at the Elements title bar, which always shows the filename of the active image. You can also right-click (Control -click on a Mac) over the image in the Photo Bin and then click **Show Filenames**. Elements displays the filename directly below each image in the Photo Bin. The Show Filenames feature toggles on or off.

Adjust the Image View

You can move an image within the window by using the Hand tool or scroll bars. The Hand tool helps you navigate to an exact area on the image.

The Hand tool is a more flexible alternative to using the scroll bars because, unlike the scroll bars, the Hand tool enables you to drag the image freely in two dimensions.

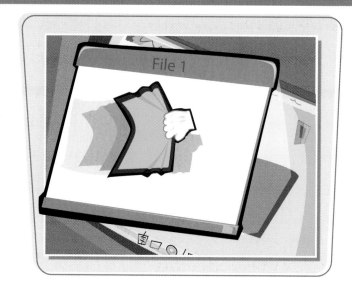

Adjust the Image View

USING THE HAND TOOL

① Click the Hand tool ().

● The ⌖ changes to ✋.

Note: For ✋ to produce an effect, the image must be larger than the image window.

② Click and drag inside the image window.

The view of the image shifts inside the window.

USING THE SCROLL BARS

1 Click and hold one of the window's scroll bar buttons (, , , or).

The image scrolls in the direction you select.

TIPS

How can I quickly adjust the image window to see the entire image at its largest possible magnification on-screen?

You have three different ways to magnify the image to its largest possible size: By double-clicking , by clicking **Fit On Screen** on the Options bar, or by clicking **View** and then **Fit on Screen** from the menu. When Elements fits the image in the work area, it maintains the image's dimensions rather than fill the entire work area.

How do I rotate an image?

To move an image vertically or horizontally, click **Image**, click **Rotate**, and then select a rotation command. To quickly reposition an image that was imported sideways, either horizontally or vertically, click **90° Left** or **90° Right**.

You can change the size of an image you import into Photoshop Elements. When adjusting sizes, keep in mind that bitmap images resize differently than vector images. Resizing a bitmap image may result in loss of image quality, but resizing a vector image does not affect image quality.

When you change an image's size, remember to resample. *Resampling* is the process of increasing or decreasing the number of pixels in an image. Decreasing pixels can improve quality while adding pixels can degrade image quality.

① Click **Image**.

② Click **Resize**.

③ Click **Image Size**.

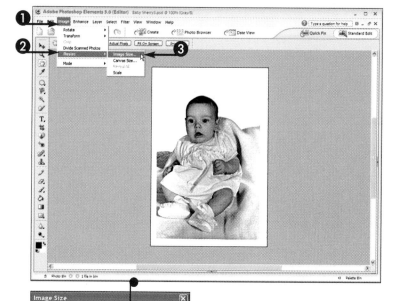

The Image Size dialog box appears listing the width and height of the image in pixels.

● To resize by a certain percentage, click here and change the units to **percent**.

④ Click the **Resample Image** option (☐ changes to ☑).

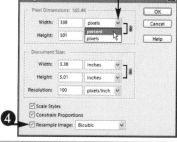

5 Type a size or percentage for a dimension.

● You can click the **Constrain Proportions** option (☐ changes to ☑) to cause the other dimension to change proportionally.

6 Click **OK**.

You can restore the original dialog box settings without exiting the dialog box by holding down Alt (option on a Mac) and clicking **Cancel**, which changes to **Reset**.

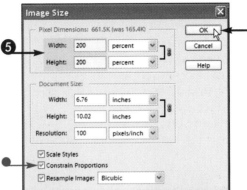

Photoshop Elements resizes the image.

In this example, the image increases in size by 200%.

Note: *Changing the number of pixels in an image can add blur. To sharpen a resized image, apply the Unsharp Mask filter as covered in Chapter 7.*

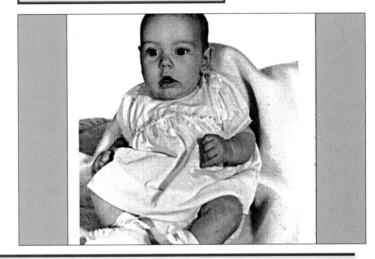

What is the difference between an image's on-screen size and its print size?

On-screen size depends only on the number of pixels that make up an image. Print size depends on the number of pixels as well as the print resolution, which is the density of the pixels on a printed page. Higher resolutions print a smaller image, while lower resolutions print a larger image, given the same on-screen size.

I do not like the new size I set. How do I undo the effect?

You can use the Undo and Redo commands in Photoshop Elements to undo an action you just performed, or redo an action you just undid. To undo an action, click the Step Backward button (🖻), or click **Edit**, and then click **Undo**. To redo the action again, click the Step Forward button (🖻), or click **Edit**, and then click **Redo**.

You can change the printed size of an image to determine how it appears on paper. Print size is also called *document size* in Photoshop Elements.

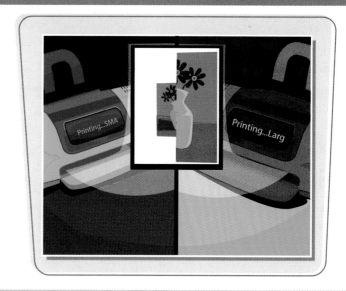

1 Click **Image**.

2 Click **Resize**.

3 Click **Image Size**.

The Image Size dialog box appears listing the current width and height of the printed image.

● You can click here to change the unit of measurement.

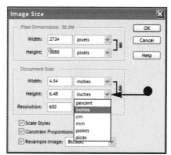

④ Type a size for a dimension.

● You can click the **Constrain Proportions** option (☐ changes to ☑) to cause the other dimension to change proportionally.

⑤ Click **OK**.

You can restore the original dialog box settings by holding down **Alt** (**option** on a Mac) and clicking **Cancel,** which changes to **Reset**.

Photoshop Elements resizes the image.

Note: Changing the number of pixels in an image can add blur. To sharpen a resized image, apply the Unsharp Mask filter as covered in Chapter 7.

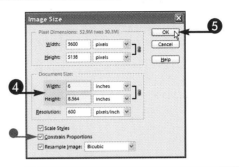

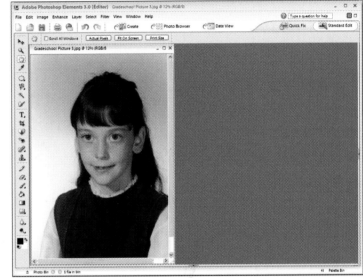

TIP

How do I preview an image's printed size?

① Click **File**.

② Click **Print**.

The Print Preview dialog box displays how the image will print on the page.

● To select another print size, click here and click a print size.

③ Click **Cancel**.

Elements exits the dialog box.

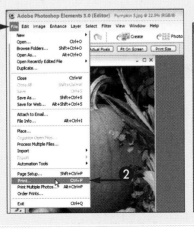

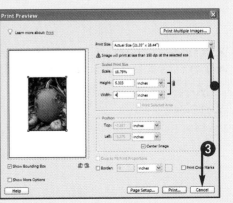

You can change the print resolution of an image to increase or decrease the print quality. The resolution, combined with the number of pixels in an image, determines the size of a printed image. The greater the resolution, the better the image looks on the printed page — up to a limit, which varies with the type of printer you use.

Change the Image Resolution

① Click **Image**.

② Click **Resize**.

③ Click **Image Size**.

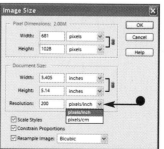

The Image Size dialog box appears listing the current resolution of the image.

● You can click here to change the resolution units.

④ Type a new resolution.

● You can click the **Resample Image** option (☐ changes to ☑) to adjust the number of pixels in your image and keep the printed dimensions fixed.

⑤ Click **OK**.

You can restore the original dialog box settings by holding down **Alt** (**option** on a Mac) and clicking **Cancel,** which changes to **Reset.**

Because the change in resolution changes the number of pixels in the image, the on-screen image changes in size while the print size stays the same.

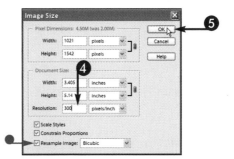

What is the relationship between resolution, on-screen size, and print size?

To determine the printed size of a Photoshop image, you can divide the on-screen size by the resolution. If you have an image with an on-screen width of 480 pixels and a resolution of 120 pixels per inch, the printed width is 4 inches.

What is a good resolution for images I intend to print out?

Picture sharpness is measured in dpi, or dots per inch. The resolution or dpi you set depends on the size of the picture. For best picture printing results with smaller pictures, such as 4 x 6 photos, make sure you use at least 240 dpi. For larger photos, such as 5 x 7 and larger, use at least 300 dpi.

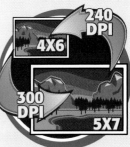

Change the Image Canvas Size

You can alter the canvas size of an image in order to change its rectangular shape or add blank space around its borders. The *canvas* is the area on which an image sits. Changing the canvas size is one way to crop an image, or add matting, which is simply blank space, around an image.

Change the Image Canvas Size

① Click **Image**.

② Click **Resize**.

③ Click **Canvas Size**.

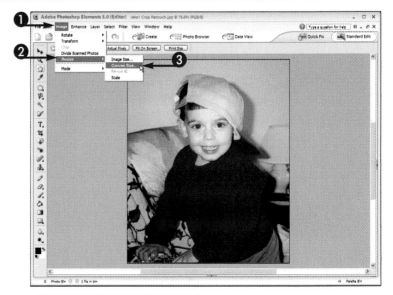

The Canvas Size dialog box displays, listing the current dimensions of the canvas.

● You can click here to change the unit of measurement.

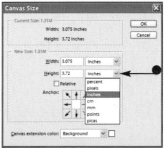

④ Type the new canvas dimensions.

● You can click an arrow () to modify in which directions Elements changes the canvas size by selecting an anchor point.

⑤ Click **OK**.

*Note: If you decrease a dimension, Elements displays a dialog box asking whether you want to proceed. Click **Proceed**.*

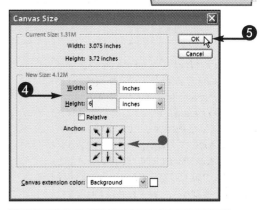

Photoshop Elements changes the image's canvas size.

Elements fills any new canvas space with the background color – in this case, white.

If you selected an anchor point, the canvas size changes equally on opposite sides.

TIPS

Why would I want to change the canvas size instead of using the Crop tool?

You may find changing the canvas size useful when you want to change the size of an image precisely. You can specify the exact number of pixels that Elements adds or subtracts around the border. With the Crop tool, you may find it more difficult to make changes with pixel precision. For more on cropping pictures, see Chapter 7.

How do I change the matte color around my canvas size?

To add a color other than the default white to your canvas, you can click the Canvas extension color in the Canvas Size dialog box. This displays a menu for choosing another color, such as black or gray. To select a color from the Elements Color Palette, click **Other** and then select a color.

Revert an Image

You can revert an image to the previously saved state. This enables you to start your image editing over.

① Click **File**.

② Click **Revert to Saved**.

Photoshop Elements reverts the image to its previously saved state.

● You can also click **Edit** and then **Undo Revert** to return to the unreverted state or click 🖻.

You can duplicate an image and apply any retouching and restoration techniques and then compare the duplicate with the original. Because you can open more than one image at a time in Photoshop Elements, you can compare the original with the edited version side-by-side.

Duplicate an Image

1 Click **File**.

2 Click **Duplicate**.

The Duplicate Image dialog box opens.

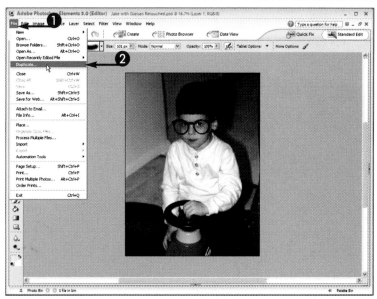

3 Type a new name for the duplicate image.

Photoshop Elements assigns a default name.

You can use the default name or change the name, if needed.

4 Click **OK**.

Photoshop Elements creates a duplicate file and places it in the workspace.

CHAPTER 4

Selection Techniques

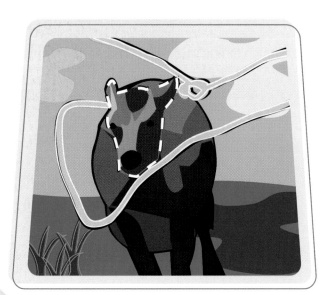

Do you want to move, color, or transform parts of your image independently from the rest of the image? The first step is to make a selection. This chapter shows you how to use the Photoshop Elements selection tools to select portions of your images for editing.

Select an Area with a Marquee 70

Select an Area with a Lasso 72

Select an Area with the Magic Wand 76

Select with the Selection Brush 78

Add to or Subtract from a Selection 80

Invert a Selection 82

Grow a Selection 83

Save and Load a Selection 84

Select an Area with a Marquee

You can select parts of an image for editing by using a marquee. Then you can make changes to the selected area using other Photoshop Elements commands. The Marquee tool includes two types of marquees: rectangular or elliptical. The rectangular marquee enables you to select square and rectangular shapes while the elliptical marquee enables you to select circular or elliptical shapes.

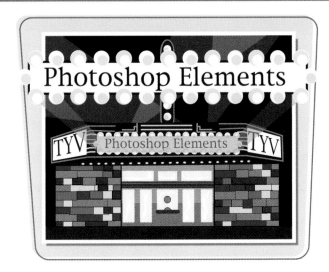

Select an Area with a Marquee

SELECT WITH THE RECTANGULAR MARQUEE

① Click the Rectangular Marquee tool (▣).

② Click and drag diagonally inside the image window.

You can hold down **Shift** while you click and drag to create a square selection.

● Photoshop Elements selects a rectangular portion of your image.

You can reposition selections by pressing the keyboard arrow keys (⬆, ⬇, ⬅, ➡).

You can deselect a selection by clicking **Select** and then **Deselect** or by clicking outside the selection area.

SELECT WITH THE ELLIPTICAL MARQUEE

1 Click and hold the (⬚).

2 Click the Elliptical Marquee tool (⬭).

You can also click ⬭ on the Options bar.

3 Click and drag diagonally inside the image window.

You can hold down **Shift** while you click and drag to create a circular selection or press **Alt** (**option** on a Mac) to draw the circle directly out from the center.

● Photoshop Elements selects an elliptical portion of your image.

You can reposition selections by pressing the keyboard arrow keys (⬆, ⬇, ⬅, ➡).

● You can deselect a selection by clicking **Select** and then **Deselect** or by clicking outside the selection area.

TIP

How do I customize the Marquee tools?

You can customize the Marquee tools (⬚ and ⬭) by using the boxes and menus in the Options bar. Marquee options only appear when you click a Marquee tool.

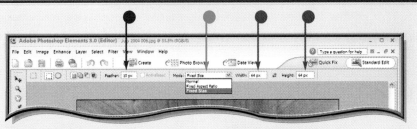

Feather

Typing in a Feather value softens your selection edge — which means that Elements partially selects pixels near the edge by building a transition between the selection and the surrounding pixels. Use a feathered selection to help you blend selections you move, cut, or copy.

Mode

The Mode list lets you define your Marquee tool as a fixed size or a fixed aspect ration.

Width and Height

You can also type in an exact width and height for your fixed size selection by entering values in the Width and Height boxes. These boxes are only operable when selecting a fixed size or fixed aspect ratio marquee.

Select an Area with a Lasso

You can create oddly shaped selections with the Lasso tools. Then you can make changes to the selected area by using other Photoshop Element commands. You can use three different types of Lasso tools: the regular lasso, the Polygonal lasso, and the Magnetic lasso.

You can use the regular Lasso tool to create freehand selections. The Polygonal Lasso tool lets you easily create a selection made up of many straight lines.

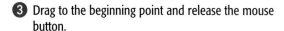

Select an Area wth a Lasso

SELECT WITH THE REGULAR LASSO

① Click the Lasso tool (⌖).

② Click and drag with your cursor (⌖) to make a selection.

● To accurately trace a complicated edge, you can magnify that part of the image with the Zoom tool (⌖).

Note: See Chapter 3 for more on the Zoom tool.

③ Drag to the beginning point and release the mouse button.

Photoshop Elements completes the selection.

SELECT WITH THE POLYGONAL LASSO

1 Click and hold .

2 Click the Polygonal Lasso tool ().

● You can also click in the Options bar.

3 Click multiple times along the border of the area you want to select.

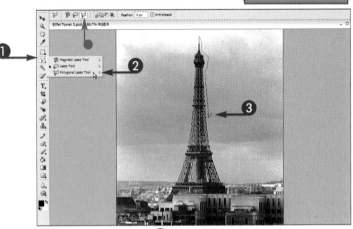

4 To complete the selection, click the starting point.

You can also double-click anywhere in the image and Photoshop Elements adds a final straight line connected to the starting point.

Photoshop Elements completes the selection.

TIPS

How do I select all the pixels in my image?

You can use the Select All command to select everything in your image. Click **Select** and then click **All**. You can also press Ctrl + A (⌘ + A on a Mac) on the keyboard. You can select all the pixels to perform edits on the entire image, such as copying the image.

Does it matter which layer I use to make a selection?

No. You can make a selection and then switch layers to apply the selection to the layer you want. To prevent yourself from accidentally making an edit on the wrong layer, you can select the layer you want to edit first before applying the selection tool. To choose a layer containing the element you want to select and edit, display the Layer palette and click the layer. To read more about using layers in Photoshop Elements, see Chapter 6.

continued

You can select elements of your image that have well-defined edges quickly and easily with the Magnetic Lasso tool. The Magnetic Lasso works best when the element you are trying to select contrasts sharply with its background.

Select an Area with a Lasso *(continued)*

SELECT WITH THE MAGNETIC LASSO

① Click and hold 📷.

② Click the Magnetic Lasso tool (📷).

● You can also click 📷 in the Options bar.

③ Click the edge of the object you want to select.

This creates a beginning anchor point.

④ Drag your cursor (📷) along the edge of the object.

The Magnetic Lasso's path snaps to the edge of the element as you drag.

To help guide the lasso, you can click to add anchor points as you go along the path.

5 Click the beginning anchor point to finish your selection.

Alternatively, you can double-click anywhere in the image and Photoshop Elements completes the selection for you.

The path is complete and the object is selected.

● This example shows that the Magnetic Lasso is less useful for selecting areas where you find little contrast between the image and its background.

TIP

How can I adjust the precision of the Magnetic Lasso tool?

You can use the Options bar to adjust the Magnetic Lasso tool's precision:

Width: 10 px   Edge Contrast: 10%   Frequency: 57

Width

The number of nearby pixels the lasso considers when creating a selection.

Edge Contrast

How much contrast is required for the lasso to consider something an edge.

Frequency

The frequency of the anchor points.

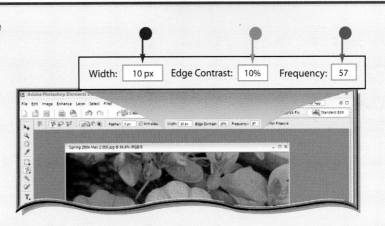

Select an Area with the Magic Wand

You can select groups of similarly colored pixels with the Magic Wand tool. You may find this useful if you want to remove an object from a background.

You can control how similar a pixel is and whether Photoshop Elements selects it by selecting an appropriate tolerance value. Tolerance controls the color range of pixels.

Select an Area with the Magic Wand

① Click the Magic Wand tool ( ).

⬡ changes to ⬡.

② Type a number from 0 to 255 into the Tolerance field.

To select a narrow range of colors, type a small number; to select a wide range of colors, type a large number.

③ Click the area you want to select inside the image.

● Photoshop Elements selects the pixel you clicked, plus any similarly colored pixels adjacent to it.

● To select all the similar pixels in the image, not just the contiguous pixels, deselect the Contiguous check box.

● This example shows a higher tolerance value, resulting in a greater number of similarly colored pixels selected in the image.

④ To add to your selection, press Shift and click elsewhere in the image.

Photoshop Elements adds to your selection.

● You can also click one of three selection buttons on the Options bar to grow or decrease the selection.

Note: *For more on these buttons, see the section "Add to or Subtract from a Selection" later in this chapter.*

With what type of images does the Magic Wand work best?

The Magic Wand tool (🖌) works best with images that have areas of solid color. The Magic Wand tool is less helpful with images that contain subtle shifts in color or color gradients. To select the greatest number of related color pixels, even in images with lots of solid color, be sure to set the Tolerance value at a higher setting.

Can I replace the selected pixels with another color?

Yes. If you press Delete, Photoshop Elements replaces the selected pixels with the current background color. If you make the selection in a layer and then delete the selected pixels, the deleted selection becomes transparent and reveals the underlying layer. For more on setting background and foreground colors, see Chapter 10. For more on layers, see Chapter 6.

Select with the Selection Brush

You can select oddly shaped areas in your image by painting with the Selection Brush. By customizing the size and hardness of the brush, you can accurately trace edges that are curved or not well defined.

Select with the Selection Brush

SELECT WITH THE SELECTION BRUSH

1 Click the Selection Brush Tool (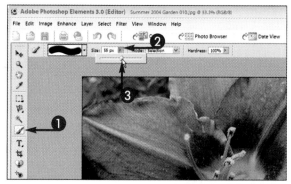).

2 Click here.

A slider (▣) appears.

3 Click and drag ▣ to specify a size.

You can also type a size.

4 Type a hardness from 0 to 100 percent.

A smaller hardness produces a softer selection edge.

5 Click here and click **Selection**.

6 Click and drag to paint a selection.

Click and drag multiple times to paint a selection over the portions you want to select.

Photoshop Elements creates a selection.

You can change the brush settings as you paint to select different types of edges in your object.

DESELECT WITH THE SELECTION BRUSH

1 Click ✎.

2 Press and hold **Alt** (**option** on a Mac).

3 Click and drag where you want to remove the selection area.

Photoshop Elements removes the selection.

TIP

How do I paint a mask with the Selection Brush?

The Selection Brush's Mask option enables you to define the area that is *not* selected in your image, also known as *masking*. One advantage of a mask is it lets you see the soft edges painted by a soft selection brush.

1 Click in the Options bar and then click **Mask**.

2 Click and drag to define the mask.

By default, the masked area shows up as a see-through red color.

To turn a painted mask into a selection, click in the Options bar and then click **Selection**.

Add to or Subtract from a Selection

You can add to or subtract from your selection by using various selection tool options.

See the previous sections in this chapter to read how to select the appropriate tool for selecting elements in your photo.

Add to or Subtract from a Selection

ADD TO YOUR SELECTION

① Make a selection using one of the selection tools.

② Click a selection tool.

This example uses the Magnetic Lasso tool.

③ Click the Add to Selection button (⬚).

④ Select the area you want to add.

⑤ Complete the selection by closing the path.

The original selection enlarges.

You can enlarge the selection further by repeating steps **2** to **5**.

You can also add to a selection by pressing **Shift** as you make your selection.

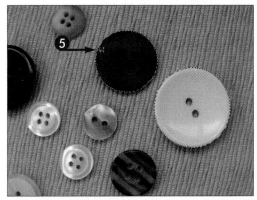

SUBTRACT FROM YOUR SELECTION

1 Make a selection using one of the selection tools.

2 Click a selection tool.

The selection in this example illustrates the use of the Elliptical Marquee tool.

3 Click the Subtract from Selection button (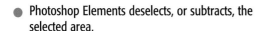).

4 Select the area you want to subtract.

● Photoshop Elements deselects, or subtracts, the selected area.

You can subtract other parts of the selection by repeating steps **2** to **4**.

You can also subtract from a selection by holding down **Alt** (**option** on a Mac) as you make your selection.

 TIPS

What tools can I use to add to or subtract from a selection?

You can use any of the Marquee, Lasso, or Magic Wand tools, discussed in previous sections in this chapter to add to or subtract from a selection. All three have Add to Selection (⬜) and Subtract from Selection buttons (⬜) available in the Options bar when you select them.

Can I move the selection marquee without moving the item selected?

Yes. Use any of the selection tools to select an area or item in the photo and then press an arrow key (⬆, ⬇, ⬅, ➡) on the keyboard to move the position of the marquee. Depending on the arrow direction you press, the selection marquee moves up, down, left, or right. Keep pressing the arrow key to move the marquee to the location you want selected. This technique is handy when you need to nudge the marquee over slightly on your selection area.

Invert a Selection

You can invert a selection to deselect what is currently selected and select everything else. This is useful when you want to select a background around an object.

See the previous sections in this chapter to select the appropriate tool for selecting elements in your image.

Invert a Selection

① Make a selection using one of Photoshop Elements' selection tools.

② Click **Select**.

③ Click **Inverse**.

Photoshop Elements inverts the selection.

In this example, everything but the large pink button is selected.

You can increase the size of your selection using the Grow command, which is useful when you want to include similarly colored, neighboring pixels in your selection.

See the previous sections in this chapter to read more about choosing the appropriate tool for selecting areas in your image.

Grow a Selection

① Make a selection using one of Elements' selection tools.

② Click **Select**.

③ Click **Grow**.

● The selection expands to include similarly colored pixels contiguous with the current selection.

To include noncontiguous pixels as well, you can click **Select** and then **Similar**.

Save and Load a Selection

You can save a selected area in your image to reuse in the same image. For example, if you spend a lot of time selecting a particular portion of your image and anticipate future edits on the same portion, you can save the selection area. By saving the selection you do not have to go through the process of selecting the area again. Instead, you can load the saved selection.

See the previous sections in this chapter to read more about choosing the appropriate tool for selecting areas in your image.

SAVE A SELECTION

① Make a selection using one of the selection tools.

② Click **Select**.

③ Click **Save Selection**.

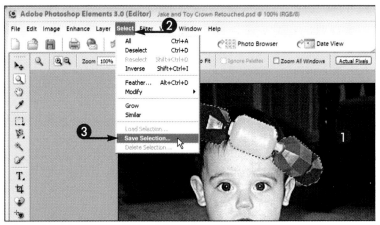

The Save Selection dialog box opens.

④ Make sure **New** is selected in the Selection field.

New is the default setting.

⑤ Type a name for the selection.

⑥ Click **OK**.

Elements saves the selection.

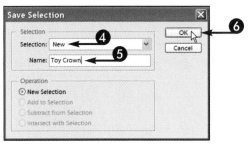

LOAD A SELECTION

1 Click **Select**.

2 Click **Load Selection**.

Note: See the subsection "Save a Selection" to save a selection.

The Load Selection dialog box opens.

3 Click here and then click the saved selection you want to load.

4 Click **OK**.

The selection appears on the image.

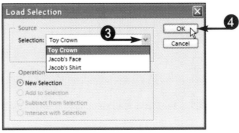

How do I delete a saved selection?

1 Click **Select**.

2 Click **Delete Selection**.

The Delete Selection dialog box opens.

3 Click here and click the saved selection you no longer want.

4 Click **OK**.

Photoshop Elements deletes the saved selection.

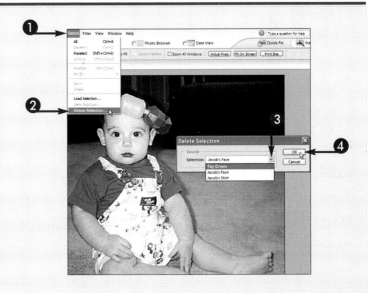

Manipulating Selections

Making a selection defines a specific area of your Photoshop Elements image. This chapter shows you how to move, stretch, erase, and manipulate your selection in a variety of ways.

Move a Selection 88

Copy and Paste a Selection..............................90

Delete a Selection 91

Rotate a Selection 92

Scale a Selection 93

Skew or Distort a Selection 94

Feather the Border of a Selection..................96

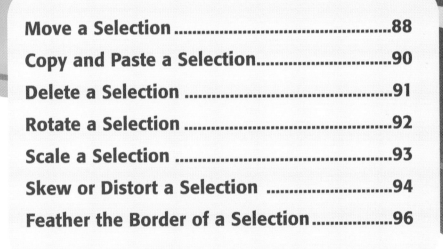

Move a Selection

You can move a selection by using the Move tool, which lets you rearrange elements of your image. You can move elements of your image either in the default background layer or in other layers you create for your image.

If you move elements on the background layer, Photoshop Elements fills in the resulting hole with the current background color. If you move elements on another layer, the resulting hole is transparent, revealing any underlying layers below. See Chapter 6 for more on layers.

Move a Selection

MOVE A SELECTION IN THE BACKGROUND

① Display the Layers palette.

② Click the Background layer.

If you start with a newly imported image, Elements makes the background layer the only layer.

Note: See Chapter 1 for more on using palettes and Chapter 6 for more on layers.

③ Make a selection with a selection tool.

Note: For more about selecting elements, see Chapter 4.

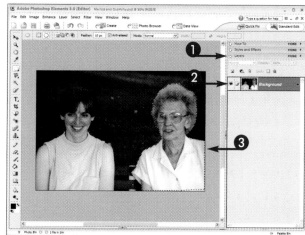

④ Click the Move tool (⊹).

⑤ Click inside the selection and drag your selection where you want it.

Photoshop Elements fills the original location of the selection with the current background color.

In this example, white is the default background color.

MOVE A SELECTION IN A LAYER

① Click a layer in the Layers palette.

Note: *See Chapter 6 for more on layers.*

In this example, the layer contains an element from another photo.

② Make a selection with a selection tool.

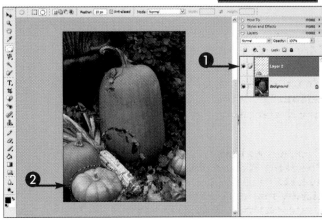

③ Click .

④ Click inside the selection and drag it where you want it.

Photoshop Elements moves the selection and fills the original location of the selection with transparent pixels.

Unlike the background — Elements' opaque default layer — layers can include transparent pixels.

TIPS

How do I move a selection in a straight line?

Hold down the **Shift** key while you drag with the Move tool (). Doing so constrains the movement of your selection horizontally, vertically, or diagonally — depending on the direction you drag.

How do I return a moved selection to its original position?

You can click the Undo button (↺) until the selected item returns to its original starting position it appeared in before you moved the selection in the layer. You can also click **Edit** and then click **Undo** to undo an action you just performed in Photoshop Elements.

Copy and Paste a Selection

You can copy a selection and make a duplicate of it somewhere else in the image. You may use this technique to retouch an element in your photo.

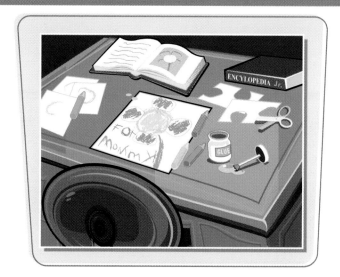

Copy and Paste a Selection

① Make a selection with a selection tool.

Note: See Chapter 4 for more on using selection tools.

② Click [✛].

⦿ You can also click **Copy** and **Paste** on the **Edit** menu to copy and paste selections.

③ Press **Alt** (**option** on the Mac) while you click and drag the selection.

④ Release the mouse button to drop the selection in place.

Photoshop Elements creates a duplicate of the selection on a new layer and moves it to the new location.

You can delete a selection to remove unwanted elements from an image. If you delete an element from the background or default layer, Elements replaces the hole with the current background color. If you delete a selection on another layer, Elements removes the selection from the layer allowing the underlying layers to show through.

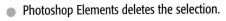

Delete a Selection

① Make a selection with a selection tool.

Note: See Chapter 4 for more on using selection tools.

② Press Delete.

● Photoshop Elements deletes the selection.

If you are working in the background layer, the empty selection fills with the background color – in this example, white, the default background color.

If you are working in a layer other than the background layer, deleting a selection turns the selected pixels transparent, and allows layers below it to show through.

Rotate a Selection

You can rotate a selection to tilt or turn an element upside down in your image. You may rotate an element to create a better composition or to correct the appearance of an element in the photo.

When you rotate a selection in the background or default layer, Photoshop Elements replaces the hole that the rotation creates with the current background color. If you rotate a selection on another layer, the underlying layers appear in the resulting hole. See Chapter 6 for more on layers.

Rotate a Selection

① Make a selection with a selection tool.

Note: See Chapter 4 for more on using selection tools.

② Click **Image**.

③ Click **Rotate**.

④ Click **Free Rotate Selection**.

⑤ Click and drag a rotation handle.

The selection rotates.

⑥ Click ✓ or press Enter (Return on a Mac) to commit the rotation.

● You can click ⊘ or press Esc (⌘ + ▪ on a Mac) to cancel.

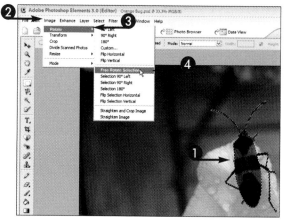

You can scale a selection to make it larger or smaller. Scaling enables you to adjust or emphasize parts of your image.

Scaling a selection on the background layer leaves a hole in the layer, which Photoshop Elements fills with the current background color. If you scale a selection on another layer, the underlying layers appear in the resulting hole. See Chapter 6 for more on layers. See Chapter 10 for more on setting a background color.

Scale a Selection

① Make a selection with a selection tool.

Note: See Chapter 4 for more on using selection tools.

② Click **Image**.

③ Click **Resize**.

④ Click **Scale**.

A box with handles on the sides and corners surrounds the selection.

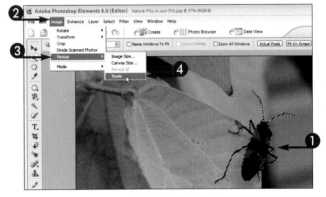

⑤ Drag a handle to scale the selection.

Drag a corner handle to scale both the horizontal and vertical axes.

Press and hold Shift to scale proportionally.

⑥ Click ☑ or press Enter (Return) to apply the scale effect.

● To cancel, you can click ◯ or press Esc (⌘ + ▢).

Photoshop Elements scales the selection.

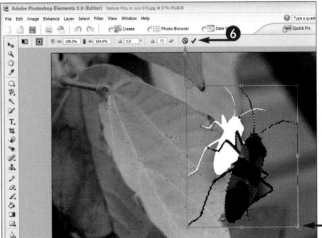

Skew or Distort a Selection

You can transform a selection using the Skew or Distort command. This lets you stretch elements in your image into interesting shapes.

Skewing or distorting a selection on the background layer leaves a hole in the layer, which Elements fills with the current background color. If you skew or distort a selection on another layer, the underlying layers appear in the resulting hole. See Chapter 6 for more on layers. See Chapter 10 for more on setting a background color.

Skew or Distort a Selection

SKEW A SELECTION

① Make a selection with a selection tool.

Note: See Chapter 4 for more on using selection tools.

② Click **Image**.

③ Click **Transform**.

④ Click **Skew**.

A rectangular box with handles on the sides and corners surrounds the selection.

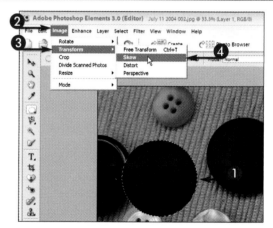

⑤ Click and drag a handle.

Photoshop Elements skews the selection.

Because the Skew command works along a single axis, you can drag either horizontally or vertically.

⑥ To apply the skewing, click ✓ or press Enter (Return).

● To cancel, you can click Ⓢ or press Esc (⌘ + .).

DISTORT A SELECTION

1 Make a selection with a selection tool.

Note: See Chapter 4 for more on using selection tools.

2 Click **Image**.

3 Click **Transform**.

4 Click **Distort**.

A rectangular box with handles on the sides and corners surrounds the selection.

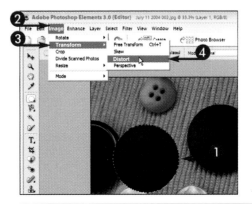

5 Click and drag a handle.

Photoshop Elements distorts the selection.

The Distort command works independently of the selection's different axes; you can drag a handle both vertically and horizontally.

6 To apply the distortion, click ✓ or press Enter (Return).

● To cancel, you can click ⊘ or press Esc (⌘ + .).

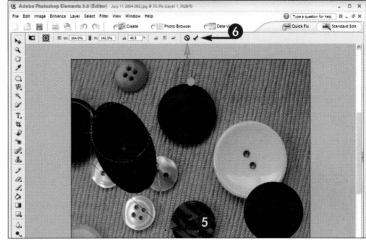

TIP

Can I perform several transforming effects at once to a selection?

The Free Transform tool scales, rotates, and skews a selection all at once. To use the tool, select the item and follow these steps:

1 Click **Image**.

2 Click **Transform**.

3 Click **Free Transform**.

4 Drag a handle on the box that surrounds the selection to transform it.

● You can switch between transformation styles by clicking these buttons.

5 To apply the transformation effect, click ✓ or press Enter (Return).

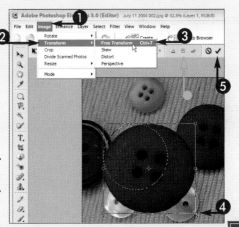

Feather the Border of a Selection

You can feather a selection's border to create soft edges. Feathering enables you to control the sharpness of the edges in a selection. You can use this technique with other layers to create a blending effect between the selected area and any underlying layers.

To create a soft edge around an object, you must first select the object, feather the selection border, and then delete the part of the image that surrounds your selection.

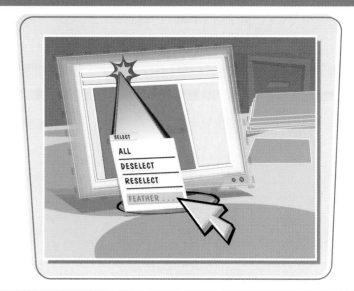

Feather the Border of a Selection

SELECT AND FEATHER THE IMAGE

1 Make a selection with a selection tool.

Note: See Chapter 4 for more on using selection tools.

2 Click **Select**.

3 Click **Feather**.

The Feather Selection dialog box appears.

4 Type a pixel value to determine the softness of the edge.

5 Click **OK**.

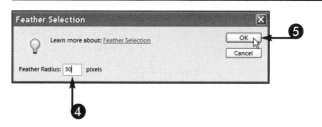

DELETE THE SURROUNDING BACKGROUND

⑥ Click **Select**.

⑦ Click **Inverse**.

The selection inverts, but remains feathered.

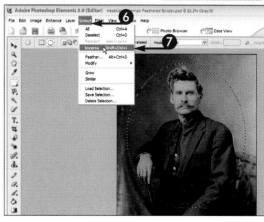

⑧ Press Delete .

You can now see the effect of the feathering.

TIPS

How do I feather my selection into a color background?

You can add a solid color fill layer to your photo and blend the feathered selection into the color layer. The layer containing the selection appears on top of the fill color layer, and the feathering technique creates a softened blend between the two layers. For more on creating a fill layer, see Chapter 6.

If I feather a selection and do not delete the surrounding area, can I still see the feathering effect?

No. To see the effect, you must remove the surrounding area either by deleting the rest of the layer or by inserting a fill color layer or another layer effect. You can also choose to hide the layer temporarily to see the effect. See Chapter 6 for more on working with layers in Photoshop Elements.

CHAPTER

6

Layer Basics

Do you want to separate the elements in your photo so that you can move and transform them independently of one another? You can do this by placing them in different layers.

Understanding Layers..100

Add Layers..102

Select a Layer..104

Hide a Layer...105

Move a Layer..106

Duplicate a Layer..107

Change Layer Stacking Order..........................108

Delete a Layer..110

Create a Layer from a Background.................111

Change the Opacity of a Layer......................112

Link Layers...113

Merge and Flatten Layers................................114

Create a Fill Layer...116

Create an Adjustment Layer...........................118

Blend Layers..120

Understanding Layers

You can use layers to edit and retouch different objects in an image. You can also use layers to combine elements from different images. An Elements image can consist of multiple layers, with each layer containing different objects in the image. By default, each image starts with one layer. You can add more layers as needed. You can see your image layers in the Layers palette.

Layer Independence

Layered image files act like several images combined into one. Each layer of an image has its own set of pixels that you can move and transform independently of the pixels in other layers. This enables you to make changes to one part of an image without affecting the rest of the image.

Apply Commands to Layers

Most Elements commands affect only the layer that you select. For example, if you click and drag using the Move tool, the selected layer moves while the other layers stay in place; if you apply a color adjustment, only colors in the selected layer change.

Manipulate Layers

By manipulating layers, you can change the appearance of objects and people in your photos. You can combine, duplicate, and hide layers in an image. You can also shuffle the order in which you stack layers, thus rearranging elements in an image. When your edits are complete, you can combine or merge the layers into one final image, thus making your changes permanent.

Transparency

Layers can have transparent areas, where the elements on the layers below can show through. When you perform a cut or erase command on a layer, the affected pixels become transparent. You can see underlying layers through the transparent pixels.

Adjustment Layers

Adjustment layers are special layers that contain information about color or tonal adjustments. An adjustment layer affects the pixels in all the layers below it. You can increase or decrease an adjustment layer's strength to get precisely the effect you want. Adjustment layers are a good way to test edits without applying them to the final image.

Save Layered Files

You can only save multilayered images in the Elements default file format, PSD. To save a layered image in another file format — for example, PICT, GIF, or JPEG — you must combine the image's layers into a single layer, a process known as *flattening*. For more information about outputting your retouched or restored photos, see Chapter 16.

Add Layers

You can create separate layers to keep elements in your image independent from one another and to retouch elements separately. You can create a new layer and add elements to it, or you can turn a selected element in your image into its own layer for editing.

When turning a selection into a layer, you can cut the selection and paste it into the new layer or copy and paste it, making a duplicate of the original element.

Add Layers

CREATE A NEW LAYER

1 Display the Layers palette.

Note: For more information on opening and using palettes and viewing the Palette Bin, see Chapter 1.

2 Click the layer above which you want to add the new layer.

3 In the Layers palette, click the Create a New Layer button (■).

● Alternatively, you can click **Layer**, click **New**, and then click **Layer**.

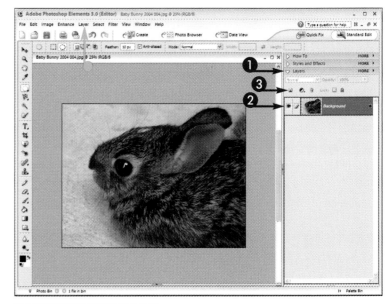

● Photoshop Elements creates a new, transparent layer with a default name.

● To name a layer, double-click the layer name in the palette, type a new name, and press Enter (Return on the Mac).

You can cut, copy, and paste selections from other layers into the new layer for editing.

Note: For more on selecting image elements, see Chapter 4.

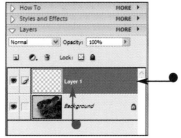

TURN A SELECTION INTO A LAYER

1 Using a selection tool, select the content you want to place in a new layer.

Note: For more on selection tools, see Chapter 4.

2 Click **Layer**.

3 Click **New**.

4 Click **Layer Via Copy** or **Layer Via Cut**.

● Photoshop Elements copies and pastes, or cuts and pastes, the selected content into the new layer.

● To view only the new layer in the workspace, click the Eye icon () next to the other layer names in the Layers palette.

Note: See the section "Hide a Layer" for more on viewing layers.

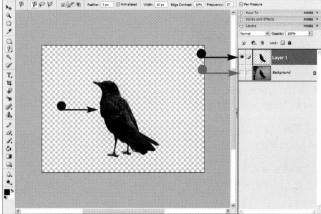

TIP

What is the background layer?

The background layer is the default bottom layer that appears when you create a new image or when you import an image from a scanner or camera. You can create new layers on top of a background layer, but not below it. Unlike other layers, a background layer cannot contain transparent pixels. You can duplicate the background layer to perform edits without affecting the original background layer. To duplicate a layer, click the background layer in the Layers palette, click **Layer**, click **New**, and then click **Layer via Copy**.

You can select a layer in the Layers palette to make changes to the layer. The Layers palette lists all the layers in your image file, including the bottommost layer, called the Background layer.

By default, all image files start with the Background layer until you add more layers for editing image elements. There is an exception – if you start a new, blank image with the File, New command, the resulting file does not use a background layer.

Select a Layer

1 Display the Layers palette.

Note: For more about opening and using palettes, see Chapter 1.

In this example, Layer 1 is selected and Layer 2 is hidden from view.

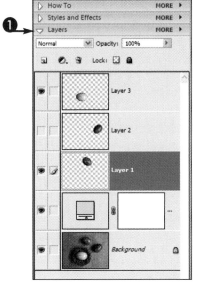

2 Click a layer.

Photoshop Elements selects the layer and you can now make changes to the layer.

In this example, Layer 2 is selected and now in view.

Note: See the section "Add Layers" earlier in this chapter to read how to add new layers and turn selections into layers.

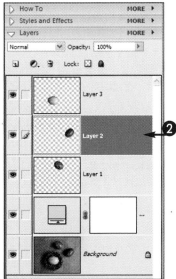

Hide a Layer

You can hide a layer to temporarily remove elements in that layer from view. Hiding a layer enables you to concentrate on other elements you want to edit.

Hidden layers do not display when you print or use the Save for Web command.

Hide a Layer

❶ Display the Layers palette.

Note: *For more about opening and using palettes, see Chapter 1.*

❷ Click a layer.

❸ Click the Eye icon (👁) for the layer.

● Photoshop Elements hides the layer and 👁 disappears.

To show one layer and hide all the others, you can press **Alt** (**option** on a Mac) and click the 👁 for the layer.

● You can click 🔒 to lock a layer and prevent accidental changes.

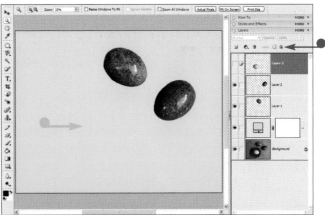

Move a Layer

You can use the Move tool to reposition the elements in one layer without moving those in other layers. You can move layers to rearrange the composition of a photo.

To rearrange composition elements, you must create a new layer out of each selected element. See the section "Add Layers" for more on how to turn a selection into a separate layer.

Move a Layer

① Display the Layers palette.

Note: For more about opening palettes, see Chapter 1.

② Click a layer.

Note: See the section "Add Layers" for more on creating layers.

③ Click the Move tool (⊹).

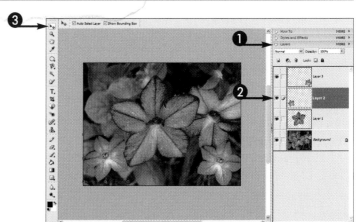

④ Click and drag inside the window.

Content in the selected layer moves.

Content in the other layers does not move.

Note: To move several layers at once, see the section "Link Layers."

By duplicating a layer, you can manipulate elements in an image while keeping a copy of their original state. For example, you can use a duplicate layer to practice making retouching or restoration edits before applying them to the original layer.

Duplicate a Layer

1 Display the Layers palette.

Note: For more about opening palettes, see Chapter 1.

2 Click a layer.

3 Click and drag the layer to ⬚.

Alternatively, you can click **Layer** and then **Duplicate Layer**, and a dialog box appears enabling you to name the layer.

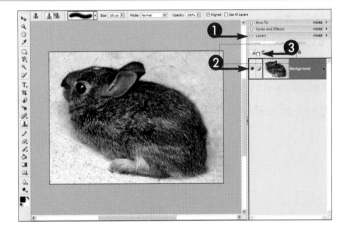

● Photoshop Elements duplicates the selected layer.

● You can see that Elements has duplicated the layer by your selecting the new layer, clicking 🔁, and clicking and dragging the layer.

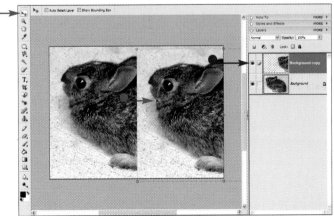

Change Layer Stacking Order

You can change the stacking order of layers to move elements forward or backward in your image.

You can use the selection tools to save different objects in your image as separate layers and then reorder their position in the image by changing the layer stacking order. To turn a selection into a layer, see the section "Add Layers" earlier in this chapter. For more on selecting items in your photos, see Chapter 4.

Change Layer Stacking Order

CHANGE ORDER WITH THE LAYERS PALETTE

① Display the Layers palette.

Note: For more about opening palettes, see Chapter 1.

② Click the layer you want to move in the layer stacking order.

In this example, the Bird layer appears on top of the stack.

③ Click and drag the layer to change its arrangement in the stack.

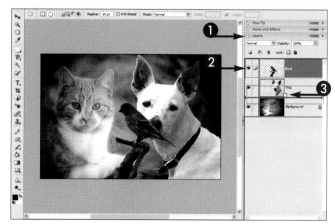

④ Release the mouse button.

● The layer assumes its new position in the stack.

● In this example, the Bird layer moves back in the stack.

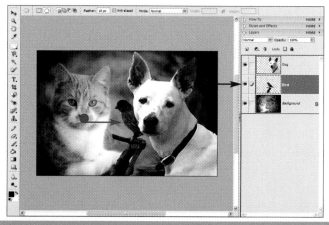

CHANGE ORDER WITH COMMANDS

1 Click a layer.

2 Click **Layer**.

3 Click **Arrange**.

4 Click the command for how you want to move the layer: **Bring to Front**, **Bring Forward**, **Send Backward**, or **Send to Back**.

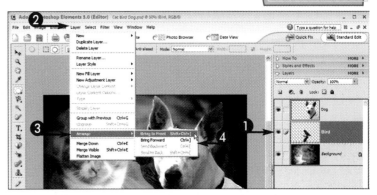

● The layer assumes its new position in the stack.

● In this example, the Bird layer moves to the top of the stack.

Note: You cannot move a layer in back of the default Background layer.

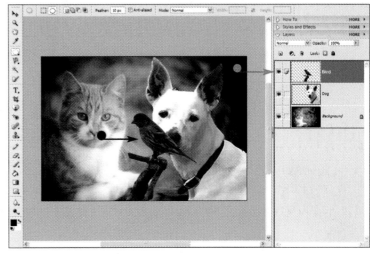

Can I use shortcuts to change the order of layers?

To move a layer	In Windows press	On a Mac press
One level up in the stack	Ctrl +]	⌘ +]
One level back in the stack	Ctrl + [	⌘ + [
To the very front of a stack	Shift + Ctrl +]	Shift + ⌘ +]
To the very back of the stack	Shift + Ctrl + [	Shift + ⌘ + [

You can delete a layer when you no longer have a use for its contents. After you delete a layer, it is permanently removed from the image file, including all the edits you made to the layer.

1 Display the Layers palette.

Note: For more about opening palettes, see Chapter 1.

2 Click the layer you want to delete.

3 Click and drag the layer to Delete Layer button ( ).

● Alternatively, you can click **Layer** and then **Delete Layer**, in which case a confirmation dialog box appears.

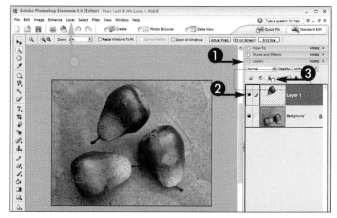

Photoshop Elements deletes the selected layer and the content in the layer disappears from the image window.

Note: You can also hide a layer. See the section "Hide a Layer" for more information.

You can turn a background layer into a layer you can edit just like any other layer in Elements. As a regular layer, you can change its stacking order.

Remember, the background layer is the image's original default layer. All images start out with a single background layer, which you cannot move in the stacking order.

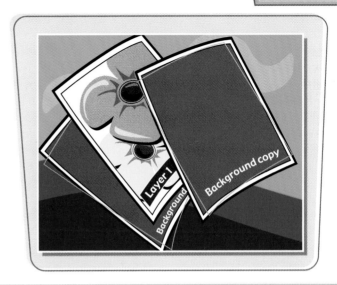

Create a Layer from a Background

1 Display the Layers palette.

Note: For more about opening palettes, see Chapter 1.

2 Click the Background layer.

3 Click **Layer**.

4 Click **New**.

5 Click **Layer From Background**.

The New Layer dialog box opens.

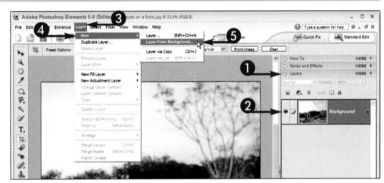

6 Type a name for the layer.

7 Click **OK**.

● Photoshop Elements converts the Background layer to a regular layer.

● To convert a layer to a background layer, click the layer and then click **Layer**, **New**, and then **Background from Layer**.

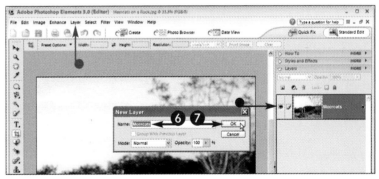

Change the Opacity of a Layer

Adjusting the opacity of a layer can let elements in the layers below show through. *Opacity* is the opposite of transparency. Decreasing the opacity of a layer increases its transparency.

1 Display the Layers palette.

Note: For more about opening palettes, see Chapter 1.

2 Click the layer you want to change.

Note: You cannot change the opacity of the default background layer.

● The default opacity is 100%, which is completely opaque.

3 Type a new value in the Opacity field.

● Alternatively, you can click here and then drag the ▢.

A layer's opacity can range from 1% to 100%.

● The layer changes in opacity.

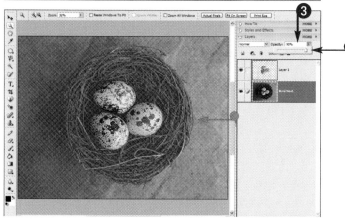

112

Link Layers

Linking causes different layers to move in unison when you move them with the Move tool. You may find linking useful when you want to keep elements of an image aligned with one another, but do not want to merge their layers. Keeping layers unmerged lets you apply effects independently of each layer.

See the section "Merge and Flatten Layers" for more on merging. For more on moving a layer, see the section "Move a Layer."

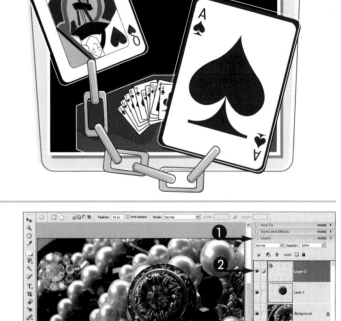

 Link Layers

① Display the Layers palette.

Note: For more about opening palettes, see Chapter 1.

② Click one of the layers you want to link.

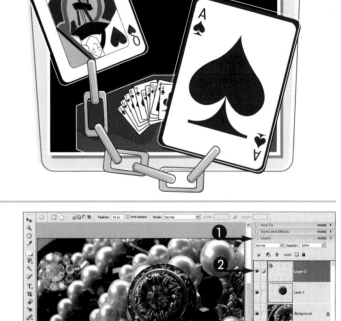

③ Click the Link box next to the other layer that you want to link.

Doing so turns on a linking icon ().

The layers link together.

Merge and Flatten Layers

Merging layers lets you permanently combine information from two or more separate layers. Flattening layers combines all the existing layers of an image into one. Use the flattening feature to create a final image that incorporates all the edits in each individual layer.

MERGE LAYERS

1 Display the Layers palette.

Note: For more about opening palettes, see Chapter 1.

2 Place the two layers you want to merge next to each other.

Note: To use palettes, see Chapter 1. See the section "Change Layer Stacking Order" to change stacking order.

3 Click the topmost of the two layers.

4 Click **Layer**.

5 Click **Merge Down**.

● The two layers merge.

Photoshop Elements keeps the name of the lower layer.

In this example, Layer 3 merged with Layer 2.

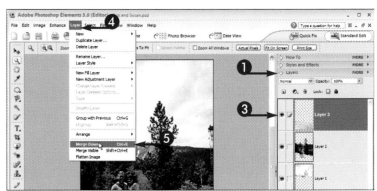

FLATTEN LAYERS

1 Click **Layer**.

2 Click **Flatten Image**.

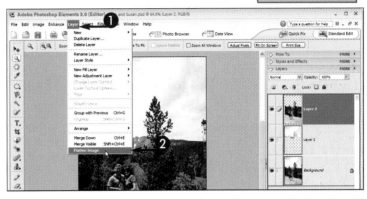

● All the layers merge into one.

Why would I want to merge layers?

Merging layers enables you to save computer memory. The fewer layers an Elements image has, the less space it takes up in RAM and on your hard drive when you save it. Merging layers also lets you permanently combine elements of your image when you are happy with how you have arranged them relative to one another. If you want the option of rearranging all the original layers in the future, save a copy of your image before you merge layers.

Can I merge layers that are not next to each other?

Yes. First, hide any layers you do not want to include in the merge. See the section "Hide a Layer" in this chapter for more on hiding layers. Next, click **Layer** and click **Merge Visible**. This command merges all the visible layers in your photo. You can use this technique to view your editing effects as they apply to certain layers and not others.

You can create a solid fill layer to place an opaque layer of color throughout your image. You can use fill layers behind layers containing selections to create all kinds of color effects in your photos.

Create a Fill Layer

① Display the Layers palette.

② Click the layer you want to appear below the solid color layer.

③ Click **Layer**.

④ Click **New Fill Layer**.

⑤ Click **Solid Color**.

You can also create a gradient or pattern fill layer by clicking **Layer**, **New Fill Layer**, and then either **Gradient** or **Pattern**.

The New Layer dialog box appears.

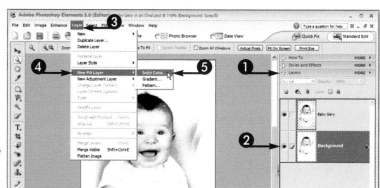

⑥ Type a name for the layer or use the default name.

● You can specify a type of blend or opacity setting for the layer.

Note: See "Blend Layers" or "Change the Opacity of a Layer" for details.

⑦ Click **OK**.

The Color Picker dialog box appears.

8 To change the range of colors that appears in the window, click and drag the slider (◁).

9 To select a fill color, click in the color area.

10 Click **OK**.

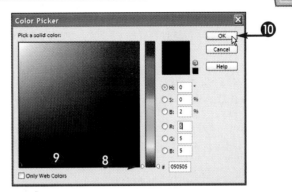

● Photoshop Elements creates a new layer filled with a solid color.

In this example, a feathered layer above the fill layer creates softened edges that give a halo effect.

Note: See Chapter 5 for more on creating a feathered border around a selection.

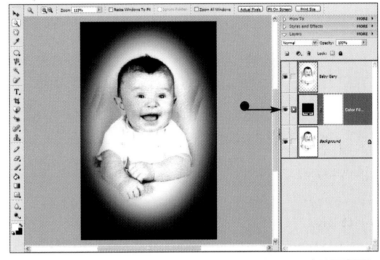

How do I add solid color to just part of a layer?

To add color to appear in a certain part of an image, first make a selection with a selection tool before creating the solid fill layer. Then apply a color fill as outlined in the preceding steps. Elements only adds color inside the selection.

What other types of fill layers can I add?

You can also create gradient fill layers, which utilize a band of colors rather than a solid fill. Or you can create a pattern fill layer, which uses a repeating pattern as a fill instead of a solid color. You can select from a variety of preset gradient effects and patterns.

Adjustment layers let you store color and tonal changes in a layer, rather than having them permanently applied to your image.

You can use adjustment layers to test an editing technique without applying it to the original layer. Adjustment layers are especially handy for experimenting with colors, tones, and brightness settings.

Create an Adjustment Layer

1 Display the Layers palette.

Note: For more about opening palettes, see Chapter 1.

2 Click a layer.

3 Click **Layer**.

4 Click **New Adjustment Layer**.

5 Click an adjustment command.

The New Layer dialog box appears.

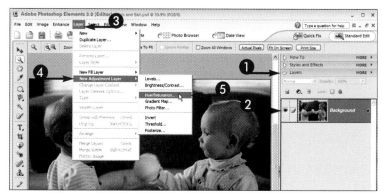

6 Type a name for the adjustment layer or use the default name.

● You can specify a type of blend or opacity setting for the layer.

Note: See the section "Blend Layers" or "Change the Opacity of a Layer" for details.

7 Click **OK**.

Photoshop Elements adds an adjustment layer to the image.

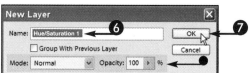

The dialog box for the adjustment command appears.

Note: *Depending on the type of adjustment layer you create, different settings appear.*

In this example, an adjustment layer is created that changes the hue and saturation.

⑧ Click and drag the sliders (🔲) or type values to adjust the settings.

You can see the adjustments take place in the workspace.

⑨ Click **OK**.

● Photoshop Elements applies the effect to the layers that are below the adjustment layer.

You can double-click the adjustment layer to make changes to the settings.

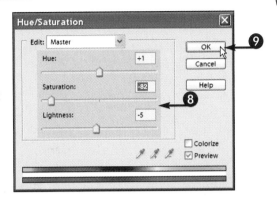

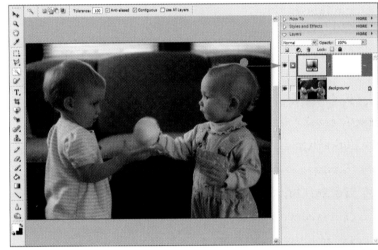

How do I apply an adjustment layer to only part of my image canvas?

Simply make a selection with a selection tool before creating the adjustment layer. Photoshop Elements turns the selected area into an adjustment layer. You can experiment with edits to the adjustment layer and any changes you make to the selection affect the underlying layers. See Chapter 4 for more on the various types of selections you can make with the Elements selection tools.

Is there a shortcut for creating an adjustment layer?

Yes. You can click the Create Adjustment Layer icon (🔲) in the Layers palette and then click the type of adjustment layer you want to create.

You can use Elements' blending modes to specify how pixels in a layer blend with the layers below it. You can blend layers to create all kinds of visual effects for your photos.

In the example shown, two photos are combined in one image file as two separate layers and blended together. You can select, copy, and paste a photo into a layer in an existing photo using the Copy and Paste commands.

Blend Layers

BLEND A REGULAR LAYER

① Display the Layers palette.

Note: For more about opening palettes, see Chapter 1.

② Click the layer that you want to blend.

③ Click here and click a blend mode.

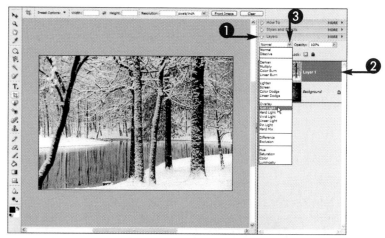

Photoshop Elements blends the selected layer with the layers below it.

This example shows the Soft Light mode, which blends a snowy forest image with an image of a cat.

BLEND AN ADJUSTMENT LAYER

1 Display the Layers palette.

Note: For more about opening palettes, see Chapter 1.

2 Click an adjustment layer that you want to blend.

3 Click here and click a blend mode.

Photoshop Elements blends the selected layer with the layers below it.

This example shows the Exclusion mode applied to a Hue and Saturation adjustment layer, which creates a photonegative effect where the layers overlap.

TIPS

What effects do some of the different blending modes have?

The **Multiply** mode darkens the colors where the selected layer overlaps layers below it. The **Screen** mode is the opposite of Multiply; it lightens colors where layers overlap. **Color** takes the selected layer's colors and blends them with the details in the layers below it. **Luminosity** is the opposite of Color; it takes the selected layer's details and mixes them with the colors below it.

How do I copy and paste a selection from another photo?

Open the photo from which you want to copy and select the item. You can press `Ctrl`+`A` (`⌘`+`A` on a Mac) to select everything, or you can press `Ctrl`+`C` (`⌘`+`C` on a Mac) to copy the selected area. Return to the photo to which you want to paste, click the layer you want to hold the pasted item, and then press `Ctrl`+`V` (`⌘`+`V` on a Mac).

CHAPTER 7

Fast Retouching Techniques

Do you need to fix a photo fast? This chapter offers you all kinds of quick techniques for making simple retouches to your digital photos.

Quick Fix a Photo 124

Remove Red Eye 126

Retouch with the Clone Stamp Tool 128

Correct a Spot 130

Remove Dust and Scratches 132

Crop an Image 134

Crop with the Cookie Cutter Tool 136

Rotate an Image 138

Straighten an Image 139

Sharpen an Image 140

Quick Fix a Photo

You can use the Quick Fix feature to make fast corrections to your photos all in one convenient window. You can adjust lighting, contrast, color, and focus. You can compare before and after previews of your adjustments. Each adjustment category includes additional settings you can change manually to achieve the correction you want to make.

The General Fixes palette includes rotation correction and the Smart Fix feature, which automatically corrects lighting, color, and contrast at the same time. The Lighting and Contrast palette fixes contrast and exposure problems. The Color Correction palette fixes color problems. The Sharpen palette sharpens photos. You can also use the Quick Fix window to crop or correct red eye problems in a photo.

Quick Fix a Photo

1 Click the **Quick Fix** button.

The Quick Fix window opens.

● You can crop or fix a red eye problem with these tools.

2 Click here and then click a view mode.

The After Only view shows the results of your changes.

The Before Only view shows only the original unedited photo.

The Before and After view shows side by side comparisons of the original and the image with changes applied.

③ Click **Auto** in the Smart Fix category.

● You can also drag the slider (⬜) to control the level of changes to the image.

● Quick Fix immediately makes adjustments to the lighting, contrast, and colors in the image.

● You can click **Reset** to reset the image to its original settings again.

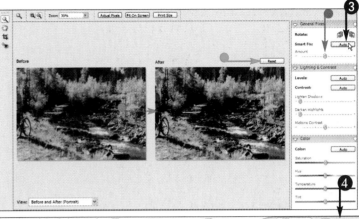

● To adjust individual categories, click an **Auto** button for the type of correction you want to make.

● You can also drag a ⬜ to adjust the setting.

● In this example, the image is sharpened and the color saturation increased.

④ Click the **Standard Edit** button.

Photoshop Elements applies the changes and returns to the default window.

Note: If you do not like the result of a Quick Fix, you can immediately click **Edit** and then click **Undo**.

 TIPS

Must I always use the Quick Fix feature to fix brightness, color, focus, and rotation problems?

No. You can make these same types of corrections using other tools in Photoshop Elements. The **Enhance** menu contains these same types of corrections, some of which open additional dialog boxes to fine-tune the adjustment.

What exactly does the Smart Fix feature do?

Smart Fix analyzes your image and attempts to make corrections in lighting, contrast, and color based on preset algorithms. Depending on the condition of the photo, the changes may be quite pronounced or barely noticeable. You can drag the Smart Fix Amount ⬜ on the General Fixes palette to control the percentage amount of change made to the color, shadows, and highlights of the image.

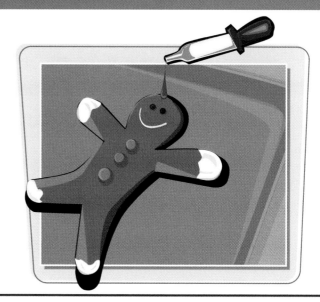

You can use the Red Eye Removal tool to remove the red eye color that a camera flash can cause. Red eye is a common problem in snapshots taken indoors with a flash. The light from the flash reflects off the back of the subject's eyes creating the red eye appearance. Using the Red Eye Removal tool, you can edit the eye to change the color hue without changing image details.

Remove Red Eye

1 Click the Red Eye Removal tool (⬚).

2 Click here and then drag the ⬚ that appears to select the percentage of correction you want to apply.

Note: You can also fix red eye problems in the Quick Fix window. See the previous section to learn more.

3 Click here and then drag the ⬚ that appears to the darkness setting you want.

④ Click and drag over the eye you want to fix.

⑤ Release the mouse button.

Photoshop Elements repairs the color.

TIP

My pet photos have a green eye problem. How do I fix this?

Like the red eye problem caused in people shots, pet shots can suffer from green or blue eye. The camera flash reflects off the back of the animal's eye creating a green glowing color effect. A quick way to remedy the problem is to use the Burn tool to darken the eye color. Follow these steps:

❶ Click the Burn tool ( ).

❷ Set any brush style and size options you want to use.

❸ Click on the area you want to darken.

Photoshop Elements darkens the area.

You can click as many times as needed to darken the eye area.

Retouch with the Clone Stamp Tool

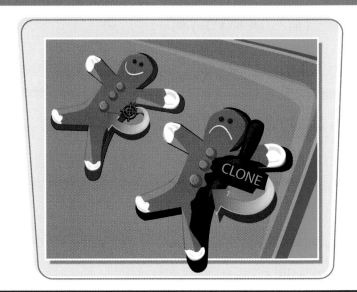

You can clean up small flaws or erase elements in your image with the Clone Stamp tool. The tool copies information from one area of an image to another. For example, you can use the Clone Stamp tool to remove unwanted blemishes of all kinds by cloning an area near the flaw and then stamping over the flaw.

Retouch with the Clone Stamp Tool

① Click the Clone Stamp tool (🏛️).

② Click here and then select a brush size and type.

● You can also set an exact brush size here.

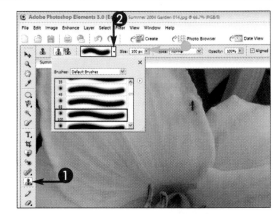

③ Press and hold **Alt** (**option** on the Mac) and click the area of the image from which you want to copy.

In this example, the Clone Stamp is used to remove an ant on the flower.

④ Click or drag on the photo flaw you want to correct.

Photoshop Elements copies the cloned area to where you click and drag.

⑤ Continue clicking new areas to clone and dragging over the flaw as many times as needed to achieve the desired effect.

The flaw disappears.

 TIPS

How can I make the Clone Stamp's effects look seamless?

To erase elements from your image with the Clone Stamp without leaving a trace, try the following:

● Clone between areas of similar color and texture.

● To apply the stamp more subtly, lower its opacity.

● Use a soft-edged brush shape.

What can I do with the Pattern Stamp?

You can use the Pattern Stamp, which shares space on the toolbox with the Clone Stamp, to paint repeating patterns on your images. To find the Pattern Stamp tool, press and hold the Clone Stamp tool (🖳), and then click Pattern Stamp (🖳) from the menu that appears. You can then select a pattern, brush style, and size and stamp the pattern on your photo.

You can use the Spot Healing Brush to quickly repair spots and other small flaws in a photo. The tool offers two healing modes, or types, from which to choose: Proximity Match and Create Texture. When you choose Proximity Match, Photoshop Elements analyzes pixels surrounding the selected area and replaces the selected spot with a patch of pixels of the same size as the selected spot. When you select Create Texture, Elements replaces the spot with a blend of surrounding pixels.

Correct a Spot

1 Click the Spot Healing Brush tool (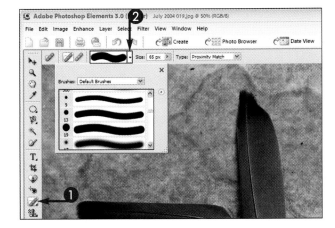).

2 Click here and then select a brush size and type.

● You can also set an exact brush size here.

3 Click here and select the type of healing effect you want to apply.

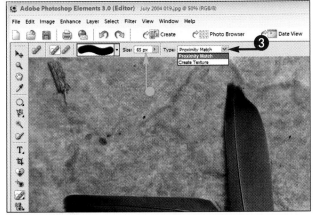

4 Click the spot you want to correct.

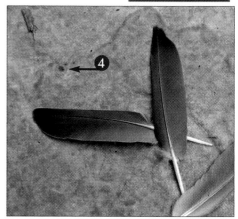

● Photoshop Elements adjusts the pixels according to the healing type you selected.

TIP

How do I correct larger areas of a photo?
You use the Healing Brush tool (🖌️) following these steps:

1 Click and hold 🖌️.

2 Click the Healing Brush tool (🖌️).

3 Adjust to the tool's settings.

4 Press and hold Alt (option on a Mac) and click the area you want to clone.

5 Drag over the area you want to fix to blend the copied pixels into the new area.

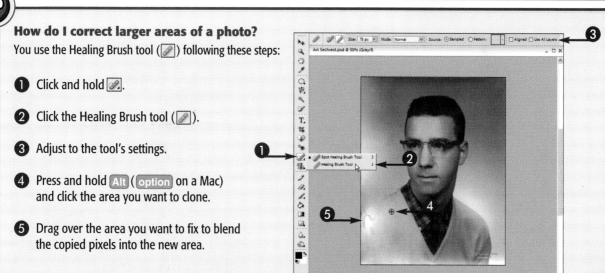

Remove Dust and Scratches

You can add slight blurring to your image to remove extraneous dust and scratches with the Dust & Scratches filter. This can help improve scans of old photographs.

Remove Dust and Scratches

① Select the layer to which you want to apply the filter.

② Select an area that has dust and scratches with a selection tool.

Note: *For more about layers, see Chapter 6. To use the selection tools, see Chapter 4.*

③ Click **Filter**.

④ Click **Noise**.

⑤ Click **Dust & Scratches**.

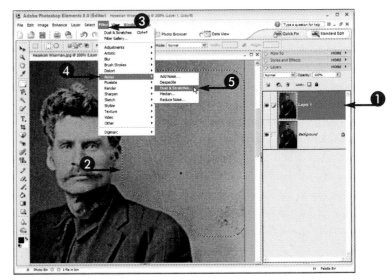

The Dust & Scratches dialog box appears.

● Photoshop Elements displays a small preview of the effect.

⑥ Click and drag the Radius slider ([⬚]) to control what size speck you consider dust or a scratch.

⑦ Click and drag the Threshold [⬚] to control how much pixels you consider dust or a scratch must differ from their surroundings.

- In this example, the Threshold value has been decreased to remove all of the selected dust.

8 Click **OK**.

- Photoshop Elements applies the filter.

TIPS

What does the Dust & Scratches filter do to areas of an image that do not have dust or scratches?

Although the intention of the Dust & Scratches filter is to remove only minor artifacts from an image, it still adds some blur wherever you apply it. For this reason, selecting areas that have dust and scratches before applying the filter is best. This prevents the filter from affecting details in an image unnecessarily.

How do I adjust the preview in the Dust & Scratches dialog box?

You can click the Minus (⊟) or Plus (⊞) buttons below the preview area to change the preview window's magnification setting. You can also move the mouse pointer over the preview area (⇖ changes to 🖑) and drag your view of the image to another area of the photo.

Crop an Image

You can use the Crop tool to quickly change the size of an image to remove unneeded space on the sides. Cropping is also a great way to edit out unwanted background elements in a photo or reposition a subject in your photo.

Another way to crop an image is by changing its canvas size. See Chapter 3 for more information about setting a new canvas size.

Crop an Image

① Click the Crop tool (⬜).

② Click and drag to select the area of the image you want to keep.

Another way to crop an image is by changing its canvas size; you do this by clicking **Image**, clicking **Resize** and then click **Canvas Size**, and then typing new dimensions for the image.

● You can set specific dimensions for a crop using the Width and Height boxes in the Options bar.

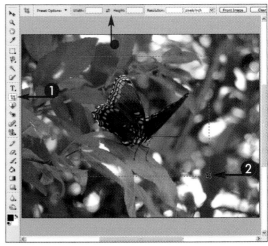

③ Click and drag the side and corner handles (⬜) to adjust the size of the cropping boundary.

You can click and drag inside the cropping boundary to move it without adjusting its size.

④ Click ✔ or press Enter (Return on a Mac).

You can also double-click inside the crop area to crop the photo.

● To exit the cropping process, you can press Esc (⌘ + . on a Mac) or click ⊘.

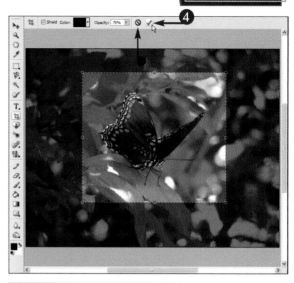

Photoshop Elements crops the image, deleting the pixels outside the cropping boundary.

Note: You can also crop images in the Quick Fix window. See the section "Quick Fix a Photo" to learn more about the window.

 TIP

How do I move my cropping area?

① Position the ⌖ over the crop area (⌖ changes to ▶).

② Click and drag the crop area over the portion of the image you want to crop.

③ Click ✔ or press Enter (Return on a Mac) to complete the crop.

Crop with the Cookie Cutter Tool

You can use the Cookie Cutter tool to crop shapes in your photos. The Cookie Cutter tool includes numerous shapes you can use to turn your subject matter into a crop of a shape, such as a heart, snowflake, and thought balloon.

The Cookie Cutter tool is especially handy when you want to crop a shape and display it on a fill layer. See Chapter 6 for more on creating a fill layer.

Crop with the Cookie Cutter Tool

① Click the layer to which you want to apply the crop.

② Click the Cookie Cutter tool (🍪).

③ Click here and then click a shape for the crop.

● To choose from more shapes, click the More button (▶) and select another shape group.

● You can click the Shape Options ▾ to change how you create the crop shape.

● The **Unconstrained** option (○ changes to ◉), which is the default setting, allows you to draw a freeform shape for the crop.

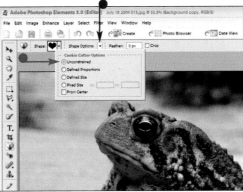

④ Click and drag the shape you want to create on the image.

Photoshop Elements crops the shape and any areas outside the shape reveal the underlying layers.

In this example, the underlying layer is a fill pattern layer.

⑤ Click ☑ or press **Enter** (**Return** on a Mac).

Photoshop Elements applies the cropping effect.

● To exit the cropping process, you can press **Esc** (**⌘**+**.**) or click **⊘**.

TIP

What other Cookie Cutter shapes can I try?

The Cookie Cutter tool includes a variety of shapes you can apply, including talk bubbles, animals, ornaments, and more. To access all the available shapes, follow these steps:

① Click the More button (⊙) on the Shape drop-down menu.

② Click **All Elements Shapes**.

The Shape menu displays all the shapes.

● You can use the scroll buttons to view the selection.

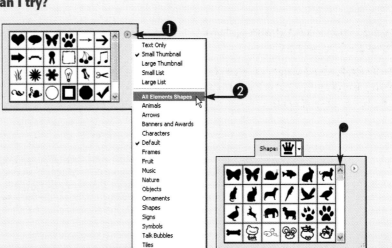

Rotate
an Image

You can rotate an image to flip it horizontally or vertically. For example, if you import or scan a horizontal image in vertically, you can rotate the image to appear in the correct direction. You can rotate an image around its center point, the very middle of the image.

You can also flip a photo to change the direction of the subject matter. Flipping an image horizontally, for example, creates a mirror opposite of the image, so everything on the right suddenly appears on the left.

Rotate an Image

① Click **Image**.

② Click **Rotate**.

③ Click **90° Left** or **90° Right** to rotate a vertical or horizontal image.

● To change subject direction, select **Flip Horizontal** or **Flip Vertical**.

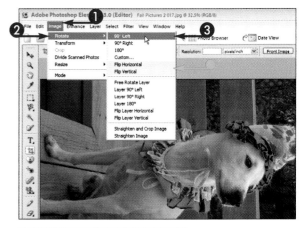

Photoshop Elements rotates the image.

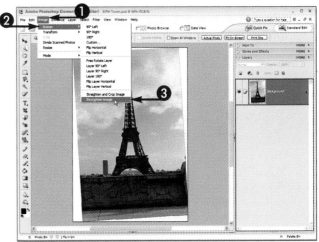

You can easily straighten an image you may have scanned in crookedly.

Straighten an Image

① Click **Image**.

② Click **Rotate**.

③ Click **Straighten Image**.

Photoshop Elements straightens the image.

You may need to crop the image to compensate for white edges created by the scan or any transparent edges created by the straightening effect.

Note: See the section "Crop an Image" for more on cropping features.

Sharpen an Image

You can use the Unsharp Mask filter to sharpen an image suffering from focus problems. The Unsharp Mask filter lets you control the amount of sharpening you apply.

To apply the filter to just part of your image, you can make the selection with a selection tool. To use the selection tools, see Chapter 4. For more about filters, see Chapter 11.

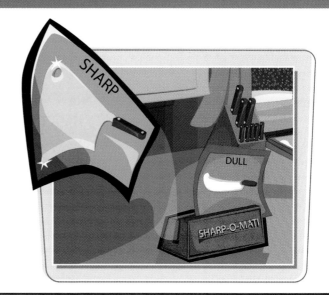

Sharpen an Image

1 Select the layer to which you want to apply the filter.

Note: For more about layers, see Chapter 6.

In this example, the image has a single background layer.

2 Click **Filter**.

3 Click **Sharpen**.

4 Click **Unsharp Mask**.

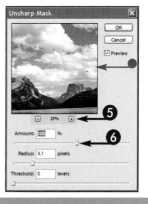

The Unsharp Mask dialog box appears.

● A small preview area displays a preview of the filter's effect.

You can click **Preview** to preview the effect in the main window (☐ changes to ☑).

5 Click ☐ or ☐ to zoom out or in.

6 Click and drag the sliders (☐) to control the amount of sharpening you apply to the image.

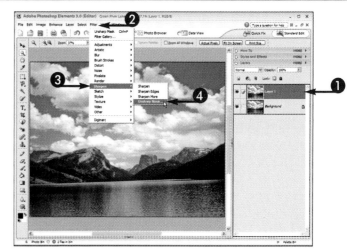

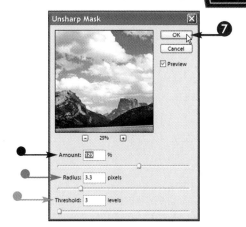

- **Amount** controls the overall amount of sharpening.

- **Radius** controls whether sharpening is confined to edges in the image (low Radius setting) or added across the entire image (high Radius setting).

- **Threshold** controls how much contrast you must have present for an edge to be recognized and sharpened.

7 Click **OK**.

Photoshop Elements applies the filter.

 TIPS

When should I apply sharpening?

Sharpening an image after you change its size is a good idea because changing an image's size adds blurring. Applying the Unsharp Mask filter can also help clarify scanned images. Although the Unsharp Mask filter cannot perform a miracle and make an unfocused image completely clear, it can sharpen up slightly blurred images or blurring caused by applying other filters.

Is the Auto Sharpen button in the Quick Fix window the same as the Unsharp Mask?

Yes. The **Auto** button on the Sharpen palette sharpens an image by a preset amount. If you use the Quick Fix window to retouch a photo, you can easily apply the Auto Sharpen command. However, you can fine-tune the sharpening effects to your liking when using the Unsharp Mask dialog box.

Enhancing Contrast and Exposure

Does your photo suffer from shadows that are too dark or highlights that are too light? Or perhaps you have an old photo in which the entire image is too faded? You can correct tone, contrast, exposure, and lighting problems using several nifty tools in Photoshop Elements. This chapter shows you how.

Adjust Levels 144

Adjust Shadows and Highlights.....................146

Change Brightness and Contrast 148

Lighten Areas with the Dodge Tool 150

Darken Areas with the Burn Tool 152

Add a Spotlight 154

Fix an Underexposed Image 156

Using the Blur and Sharpen Tools................158

Adjust Levels

You can fine-tune shadows, highlights, and tones in between using the Levels dialog box. Using Input sliders for light, dark, or average tones, you can manipulate the tonal qualities and color balance of an image to achieve just the right look for your photo. You can use the Output sliders to adjust contrast.

You can adjust shadows and highlights for the entire image or you can apply the adjustments to a selection or layer in the image. For more on selecting portions of your photos for editing, see Chapter 4. See Chapter 6 for working with layers.

Adjust Levels

① Click **Enhance**.

② Click **Adjust Lighting**.

③ Click **Levels**.

If you want to apply changes to a selection or layer, select the layer or create the selection before activating the command.

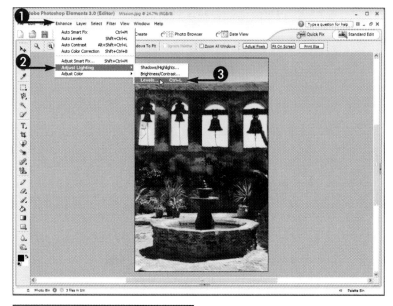

The Levels dialog box opens.

④ Make sure the **Preview** option is selected (☐ changes to ☑).

The Preview option lets you see your adjustments as you make them.

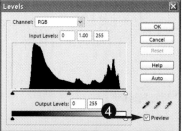

⑤ Click and drag ■ to adjust shadows.

⑥ Click and drag ■ to adjust midtones in the image.

⑦ Click and drag □ to adjust highlights in the image.

● Photoshop Elements immediately previews adjustments to the image in the workspace.

⑧ Click and drag ■ or □ to adjust the range of shadows and highlights.

⑨ Click **OK**.

Photoshop Elements applies the adjustments.

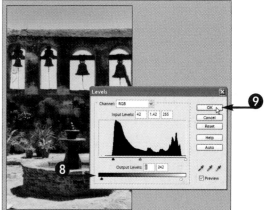

TIPS

How do you adjust the brightness levels of an image automatically?

Click **Enhance** and click **Auto Levels**. Photoshop Elements sets the lightest pixels to white and the darkest pixels to black, and then redistributes the values proportionately throughout the rest of the image. You can use the Auto Levels command to make immediate corrections to shadows, midtones, and highlights.

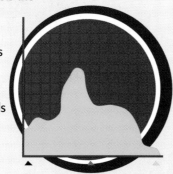

Can I tell Photoshop Elements which pixels to use as the darkest and brightest points in my image?

Yes. The Levels dialog box includes three Eyedropper tools, one for dark (✐), midtone (✐), and light tones (✐). You can click the Eyedropper tool (✐) for the tone you want to set and then click on the pixels in the image that match the dark, midtone, or light tones you want to target in the image.

Adjust Shadows and Highlights

You can use the Shadows and Highlights feature to make quick adjustments to the shadows and highlights in your photos. This feature makes adjustments to light and dark pixels in your photo. By default, when you first open the Shadows and Highlights dialog box, Photoshop Elements lightens shadows by 50%. You can make further adjustments to the shadow, highlights, and midtone using the sliders.

You can adjust shadows and highlights for the entire image or you can apply the adjustments to a selection or layer in the image. See Chapter 4 for selecting portions of your photos for editing. See Chapter 6 for working with layers.

Adjust Shadows and Highlights

① Click **Enhance**.

② Click **Adjust Lighting**.

③ Click **Shadows/Highlights**.

If you want to apply changes to a selection or layer, select the layer or create the selection before activating the command.

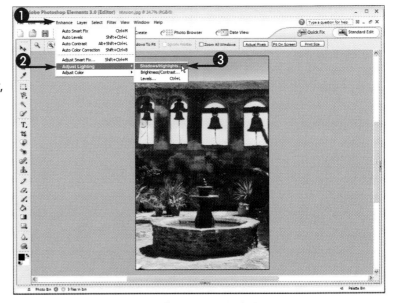

The Shadows/Highlights dialog box opens.

④ Make sure the **Preview** option is selected (☐ changes to ☑).

The Preview option lets you see your adjustments as you make them.

You can turn the preview off to see what your photo looks like without the adjustments.

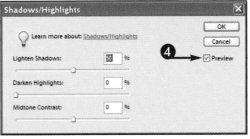

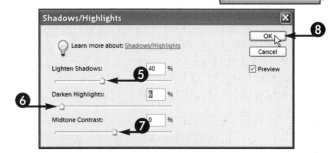

5 Click and drag 🔲 to lighten shadows in the image.

6 Click and drag 🔲 to darken highlights in the image.

7 You can drag the 🔲 to adjust midtone contrast in the image.

8 Click **OK**.

Photoshop Elements applies the adjustments.

TIPS

How do I cancel my adjustments without exiting the Shadows/Highlights dialog box yet?

If you press and hold the **Alt** (**option** on a Mac) key while clicking **Cancel (Cancel** changes to **Reset**). Click **Reset** to reset the dialog box to its original default settings.

When I reopen the Shadows/Highlights dialog box, Elements immediately adjusts my photo again. Why?

The Shadows/Highlights filter is set to automatically lighten shadows by 50%. When you reopen the dialog box to tweak the settings again, Photoshop Elements reapplies the default settings to the current photo. You can drag the sliders to adjust the settings.

Change Brightness and Contrast

You can use the Brightness/Contrast dialog box as another tool for adjusting brightness and contrast levels in a photo or a selected portion of a photo. Brightness refers to the intensity of the lighter pixels in an image. Contrast refers to the differences between dark and light areas in an image. High contrast images, for example, consist of a greater number of black and white areas, while a low contrast image displays many similar shades of gray.

For more complex adjustments of tonal qualities in an image, use the Levels dialog box. See the section "Adjust Shadows and Highlights" for more information.

Change Brightness and Contrast

① Click **Enhance**.

② Click **Adjust Lighting**.

③ Click **Brightness/Contrast**.

The Brightness/Contrast dialog box appears.

If you want to apply changes to a selection or layer, select the layer or create the selection before activating the command.

● The Preview check box is activated by default.

④ Click and drag the Brightness slider (▢) to adjust brightness.

Drag the ▢ to the right to lighten the image.

Drag the ▢ to the left to darken the image.

● You can also type a number from 1 to 100 to lighten the image or from −1 to −100 to darken the image.

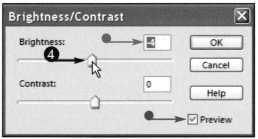

5 Click and drag the Contrast slider (◻) to adjust contrast.

Drag the ◻ to the right to increase contrast.

Drag the ◻ to the left to decrease contrast.

● You can also type a number from 1 to 100 to increase contrast or from –1 to –100 to decrease contrast.

6 Click **OK**.

Photoshop Elements applies the adjustments to the image, selection, or layer.

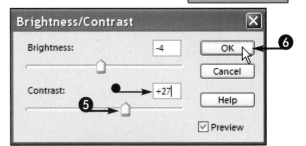

TIPS

How can I adjust the contrast of an image automatically?

You can click **Enhance** and click **Auto Contrast** and Photoshop Elements automatically converts light and dark pixels for you. The Auto Contrast feature converts the very lightest pixels in the image to white and the very darkest pixels to black. Unlike the Brightness and Contrast dialog box, you cannot fine-tune the contrast settings with Auto Contrast.

Does Elements offer a tool for evaluating tones in an image?

Yes. You can use the Histogram palette to evaluate tonal qualities in your images. Click **Window**, and then **Histogram** to open the palette. The Histogram is a graphical representation of the light and dark pixels in an image plotted out in terms of intensity. The more intense the grouping of pixels is, the taller the histogram reading for that tonal area of the image.

Lighten Areas with the Dodge Tool

You can use the Dodge tool to quickly brighten a specific area of an image. *Dodge* is a photographic term that describes the diffusing of light when developing a film negative. For example, you can tweak a dark area of an image by brushing over the area with the Dodge tool.

You can fine-tune the effects of the Dodge tool by specifying which tones to correct — either midtones, shadows, or highlights. You can also specify the strength of the lightening effect by selecting an exposure setting.

Lighten Areas with the Dodge Tool

① Click and hold the Sponge tool ().

The Dodge tool shares space with the Sponge and Burn tools on the toolbox.

② Click the Dodge tool ().

③ Click here and then click the brush that you want to use.

● You can also select an exact brush size here.

- You can click here to select the range of tones you want to affect.

- You can click here to select the tool's exposure, or strength.

④ Click and drag the cursor () over the area that you want to lighten.

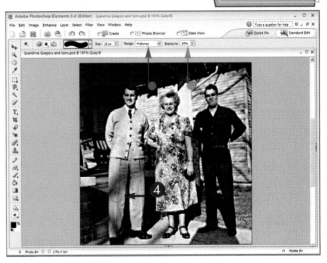

- Photoshop Elements lightens the area.

  If you continue to click or click and drag over an area, the area is lightened more with each application of the tool.

  In this example, the shadows of tree branches are completely removed from the subject.

 TIPS

Is there a way to gradually brighten the area?

If you set the Exposure level to a low value setting, you can drag repeatedly over the area you want to correct to gradually brighten the area. In this example, a cluster of grapes in the bottom photo is gradually lightened to stand out from the rest of the grapes in the photo.

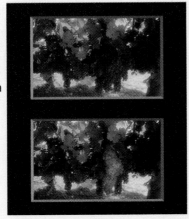

How can I add extra highlights to the lighted area of an object?

Applying the Dodge tool with the Range set to Highlights offers a useful way to add highlights to lighted areas of an object in your image. Likewise, you can use the Burn tool (🖐) with the Range set to Shadows to add shadows to the shaded side of an object. For more on the Burn tool, see the section "Darken Areas with the Burn Tool."

151

Darken Areas with the Burn Tool

You can use the Burn tool to darken a specific area of an image. *Burn* is a photographic term that describes the focusing of light when developing a film negative. For example, you can tweak a bright area of an image by brushing over the area with the Burn tool.

You can fine-tune the effects of the Burn tool by specifying which tones to correct – either midtones, shadows, or highlights. You can also specify the strength of the darkening effect by selecting an exposure setting.

Darken Areas with the Burn Tool

① Click ▣ or ▣, whichever tool is showing.

The Burn tool shares space with the Sponge and Dodge tools on the toolbox.

② Click the Burn tool (▣).

③ Click here and then click the brush that you want to use.

● You can also select the range of colors you want to affect and the tool's exposure, or strength.

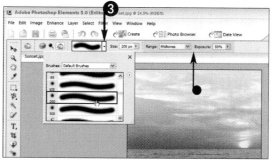

4 Click and drag the cursor (○) over the area that you want to darken.

Photoshop Elements darkens the area.

● If you continue to click or click and drag over an area, the area is darkened more with each application of the tool.

In this example, the sun area is darkened.

TIP

How do I invert the bright and dark colors in an image?

You can apply the Invert filter to make the image look like a film negative. Bright colors become dark, and vice versa. For more on Photoshop Elements filters, see Chapter 11. To apply the Invert filter, follow these steps:

1 Click **Filter**.

2 Click **Adjustments**.

3 Click **Invert**.

Photoshop Elements inverts the image.

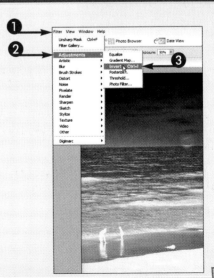

Add a Spotlight

You can use Photoshop Elements' Lighting Effects filters to create the illusion of spotlights, omni, and directional lights in an image. Lighting effects are a good way to create ambiance in your images. Elements offers 17 different light styles you can try. After you assign a light style, you can control the direction of the light source and the focus of the beam.

Omni lights shine directly over an image.
Spotlights create an elliptical beam of light.
Directional lights shine light from one angle.

Add a Spotlight

1 Select the layer to which you want to apply the filter.

Note: For more about layers, see Chapter 6.

2 Click **Filter**.

3 Click **Render**.

4 Click **Lighting Effects**.

The Lighting Effects dialog box appears.

● Photoshop Elements displays a small preview of the effect.

5 Click here and then click a lighting style.

Note: Some light styles utilize multiple lights; you must position each light in the set and adjust the settings individually.

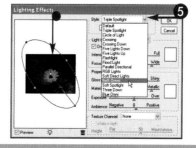

● Optionally, you can click here and click a lighting type.

6 Adjust the position and shape of the lighting by clicking and dragging the handles in the preview window.

● You can click and drag the center point to change where the light is centered.

7 Click and drag the Intensity slider (△) to control the light intensity.

8 Click **OK**.

Photoshop Elements applies the filter.

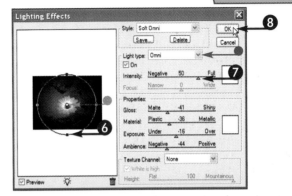

TIP

What is a lens flare, and how can I add it to an image?

Lens flare is the extra flash of light that sometimes appears in a photo when too much light enters a camera lens. Photographers try to avoid this effect, but if you want to add it, you can use the Lens Flare filter. The effect can make your digital image look more like an old-fashioned photograph. To apply the filter:

1 Click **Filter**.

2 Click **Render**.

3 Click **Lens Flare**.

The Lens Flare dialog box opens.

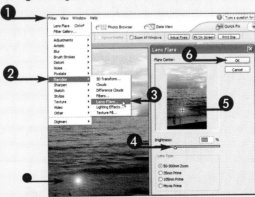

4 Drag the 🔲 to control the brightness.

5 Drag the ✛ to position the lens flare in your image.

6 Click **OK**.

● Photoshop Elements adds the lens flare effect.

Fix an Underexposed Image

You can use blending modes and layers to build and improve image lighting in underexposed images. The Multiply blending mode creates intense, dark colors, while the Screen mode lightens colors by blending them. By combining the two modes, you can modify the light in an image.

You use blending modes in conjunction with Levels Adjustment layers to fine-tune the light and dark tones in an underexposed image. You may need to experiment with the number of layers and blending modes to achieve the right effect for your own images.

Fix an Underexposed Image

① Add three Levels Adjustment layers to the Layers palette.

Note: Your own photo may require more or fewer Adjustment layers and blending modes to achieve the look you want.

Note: For more about adding layers, see Chapter 6.

② Click the first Adjustment layer.

③ Click here and then click **Multiply**.

The Multiply mode multiplies the image's base colors, resulting in more intense, darker colors.

④ Click the second Adjustment layer.

⑤ Click here and then click **Screen**.

The Screen mode produces a lighter overall color by blending the layers.

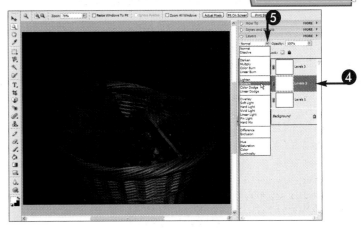

⑥ Double-click the third Adjustment layer's Levels thumbnail.

The Levels dialog box opens.

⑦ Drag the Highlights slider △ to lighten the image.

⑧ Click **OK**.

Photoshop Elements applies the adjustments.

Note: *You may need to tweak different settings to create the desired effect for your photo.*

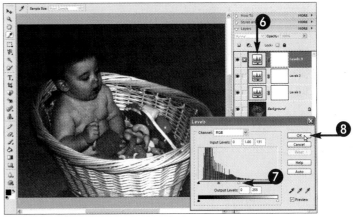

 TIPS

Can I use the Brightness and Contrast feature to fix an exposure problem?

Although the name implies corrections for image brightness, the Brightness and Contrast filter does not necessarily correct overly light or overly dark images. Raising brightness values in an image makes all the pixels lighter, while lowering the values makes all the pixels darker. For most photos, you do not need to adjust all the pixels, just those affected by the exposure problem. See the section "Change Brightness and Contrast" for more about the Brightness and Contrast filter.

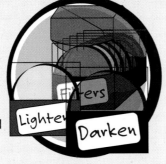

How do I fix an overexposed photo?

Depending on the amount of overexposure, you can use the Levels dialog box to make adjustments to the midtones, shadows, and highlights in your photo. By subtracting light from the image, you can make subtle corrections to an overexposed snapshot. See the section "Adjust Levels" for more information.

Using the Blur and Sharpen Tools

You can sharpen or blur specific areas of your image with the Sharpen and Blur tools. This allows you to emphasize or de-emphasize objects in a photo. You can use the Blur tool to blur away tiny spots, specks, and other small flaws in your photos. You can use the Sharpen tool to sharpen up the edges of an object.

You can blur or sharpen the entire image by using one of the Blur or Sharpen filters located in Elements' Filter menu. See Chapter 11 for more information.

Using the Blur and Sharpen Tools

USING THE BLUR TOOL

1 Click the Blur tool (⬛).

The Blur tool shares space on the toolbox with the Sharpen and Smudge tools.

2 Click here and then click the brush that you want to use.

● To change the strength of the tool, type a value from 1% to 100% or drag the ⬛.

3 Click and drag ◯ to blur an area of the image.

Photoshop Elements blurs the area.

USING THE SHARPEN TOOL

1 Click the Sharpen tool ().

The Sharpen tool shares space on the toolbox with the Blur and Smudge tools.

2 Click here and then click the brush that you want to use.

● To change the strength of the tool, type a value from 1% to 100%.

3 Click and drag ○ to sharpen an area of the image.

Photoshop Elements sharpens the area.

What is the Smudge tool?

The Smudge tool () is another tool you can use to create interesting effects in your photos. The Smudge tool shares space with the Blur and Sharpen tools on the toolbox. It simulates dragging a finger through wet paint, shifting colors and blurring your image.

Is there a filter I can use to sharpen or blur an entire image?

Yes. Photoshop Elements includes a sharpening filter, called the Unsharp Mask, as well as several other sharpening filters you can use to sharpen the appearance of pixels in a photo. For more on sharpening an image, see Chapter 7. You can also select from several blurring filters, including the Gaussian Blur, to make your image appear blurry. For more on blurring an image, see Chapter 11.

Enhancing Colors

Do your photos suffer from faded colors or unattractive color casts? This chapter shows you how to use the tools in Photoshop Elements to add, remove, and shift colors to correct color problems in your images.

Adjust Hue and Saturation 162

Adjust Color with the Sponge Tool 164

Correct Color with Color Variations 166

Replace a Color 168

Equalize Colors 170

Posterize Colors 171

Boost Colors with the Multiply

    Blending Mode 172

Turn a Color Photo into

    Black and White 174

Add Color to a Black and White Photo 176

Adjust Hue and Saturation

You can retouch the color in a photo by changing the hue or saturation. For example, if some colors appear overly bright, you can retouch them by adjusting the Hue, Saturation, or Lightness. You change the hue to shift the component colors of an image. You change the saturation to adjust the color intensity in an image. You change the lightness setting to control the brightness level of image colors.

If you make a selection before performing the Hue/Saturation command, you only affect the selected pixels. Similarly, if you have a multilayered image, your adjustments only affect the selected layer. See Chapter 4 for making selections and Chapter 6 for more on layers.

① Click **Enhance**.

② Click **Adjust Color**.

③ Click **Adjust Hue/Saturation**.

    To apply the feature to a particular layer, first select the layer before opening the dialog box.

Note: See Chapter 6 to read more about layers.

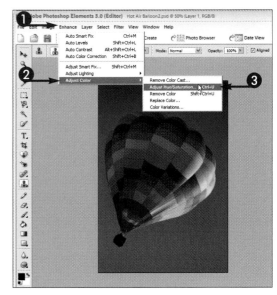

    The Hue/Saturation dialog box appears.

④ To display your adjustments in the image window as you make them, click the **Preview** option (☐ changes to ☑).

⑤ Click and drag the Hue slider (◻) to shift the colors in the image.

● To adjust just one color channel, click here and select a channel.

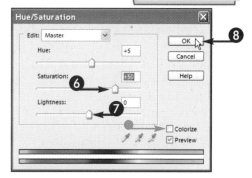

6️⃣ To increase or decrease the intensity of the color, click and drag the Saturation slider (🔲) right or left respectively.

⦿ Clicking the **Colorize** option (🔲 changes to ☑) turns the image – even a grayscale one – into a one-color, image.

7️⃣ Click and drag the Lightness slider (🔲) to shift the relative lightness or darkness of the colors.

8️⃣ Click **OK**.

Photoshop Elements makes the color adjustments to the image.

🅣🅘🅟

Can I tell Photoshop Elements to correct the color automatically?

Yes. The Auto Color Correction command adjusts the photo based on contrast and color mix by mapping the darkest and lightest pixels in the image. Follow these steps to apply the command:

1️⃣ Click the layer you want to adjust.

2️⃣ Click **Enhance**.

3️⃣ Click **Auto Color Correction**.

Photoshop Elements immediately adjusts the image colors.

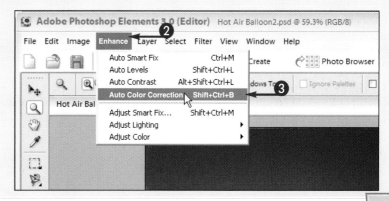

Adjust Color with the Sponge Tool

You can use the Sponge tool to make simple adjustments to the color saturation or color intensity of a specific area of an image. For example, you may need to make a person's clothing appear more colorful or tone down an element that is too colorful in an image.

Adjust Color with the Sponge Tool

DECREASE SATURATION

1 Click the Sponge tool ().

The Sponge tool shares space with the Dodge and Burn tools on the toolbox. You may need to press and hold a tool and then select it from the menu.

2 Click the brush style you want to use.

● You can click here and then click a brush style.

● You can also drag the to set a brush size.

3 Click here and then select **Desaturate**.

4 Click and drag the mouse (○) to decrease the saturation of an area of the image.

In this example, a flower petal is desaturated of its color.

INCREASE SATURATION

1 Perform steps **1** to **2** on the previous page.

2 Click here and then select **Saturate**.

3 Click and drag ○ to increase the saturation of an area of the image.

● You can adjust the strength of the Sponge tool by changing the Flow ▢ from 1% to 100%.

In this example, a portion of the butterfly's wing is saturated with color.

What does the Flow setting do?

When you click the Sponge tool (▢), the Options bar shows a Flow ▢ you can use to control the pressure setting of the saturation effect. You can set the Flow anywhere from 1% to 100%, controlling how much the sponge saturates or desaturates the pixels in your image. Start with the 50% Flow setting and then experiment with increasing or decreasing the percentage to get just the right amount of control you want.

Is there a key to finding the right brush style and size?

Picking the right tool for the job is helpful in performing edits in Photoshop Elements. The Brushes palette displays a variety of brush styles, ranging from solid edges to soft edges to airbrushes. To blend your sponging effect into the rest of the surrounding pixels, select a soft edge brush style or an airbrush style. To make your sponging edit appear in more detail, use a hard edge brush style. You can select any brush style and then use the Size ▢ on the Options bar to set a brush size for the type of edit you want to make.

Correct Color with Color Variations

You can use the Color Variations feature to quickly fix color casts and other color problems in a photo. Color casts result from unfavorable lighting situations. For example, when you shoot a subject under fluorescent lights, your photograph may take on a greenish color. Color Variations offers you a user-friendly interface with which to make color adjustments before applying the changes to the image or layer.

If you make a selection before performing the Color Variations command, you only affect the selected pixels. Similarly, if you have a multilayered image, your adjustments only affect the selected layer. See Chapter 4 to make a selection and Chapter 6 for more on layers.

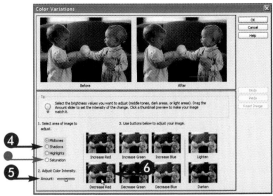

Correct Color with Color Variations

① Click **Enhance**.

② Click **Adjust Color.**

③ Click **Color Variations**.

To apply color corrections to a particular layer, first select the layer before opening the dialog box.

Note: For more about layers, see Chapter 6.

The Color Variations dialog box appears.

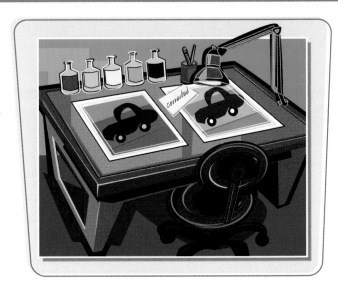

④ Select a tonal range to apply effects to the different tones of your image (○ changes to ◉).

● Alternatively, you can click **Saturation**, or strength of color (○ changes to ◉).

⑤ Click and drag ▣ left to make small adjustments or right to make large adjustments.

⑥ To add or subtract a color to your image, click one of the thumbnails.

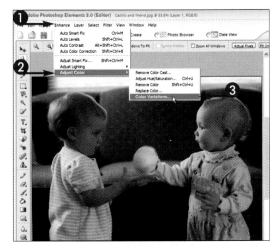

- The result of the adjustment shows up in the After preview.

  To increase the effect, you can click the thumbnail again.

- You can increase the brightness by clicking **Lighten**.

- You can decrease the brightness of the image by clicking **Darken**.

⑦ Continue adjusting other tonal ranges as needed.

⑧ Click **OK**.

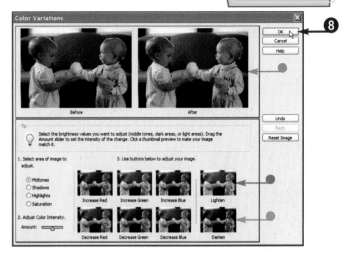

Photoshop Elements makes the color adjustments to the image.

In this example, the subjects previously suffered from a pinkish color cast caused by indoor lights, but with a few adjustments in the Color Variations dialog box, the subjects now display better color balance.

TIP

How can I undo color adjustments while using the Variations dialog box?

Increase thumbnail
Click one of the **Increase** thumbnail images to intensify a color.

Decrease thumbnail
Click the corresponding **Decrease** thumbnail image below it to undo or diminish the color effect.

Undo button
Click **Undo** to cancel the last color adjustment.

Reset Image button
Click **Reset Image** to revert the image to its original state — before you opened the dialog box.

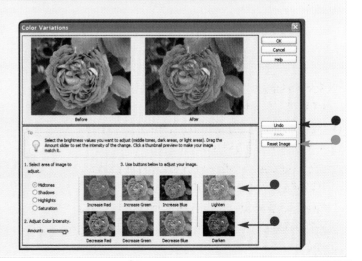

The Replace Color command lets you select one or more colors in your image and then change them using hue, saturation, and lightness controls.

If you make a selection before performing the Replace Color command, you only affect the selected pixels. Similarly, if you have a multilayered image, your adjustments only affect the selected layer. See Chapter 4 to make a selection and Chapter 6 for more on layers.

Replace a Color

① Click **Enhance**.

② Click **Adjust Color**.

③ Click **Replace Color**.

● To apply color corrections to a particular layer, first select the layer before opening the dialog box.

Note: See Chapter 6 to read more about layers.

The Replace Color dialog box appears.

④ Click the **Image** preview option (○ changes to ◉).

If you are editing a selection, click the **Selection** preview option (○ changes to ◉).

⑤ Click in the image to select a color to replace.

⑥ Click and drag ▣ to specify the Fuzziness, which controls the degree of tolerance for related colors included within the image or selection.

Dragging to the right selects more color while dragging to the left selects less color.

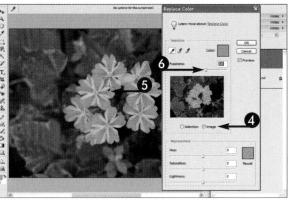

7 Click and drag the transform sliders () to change the colors inside the selected area.

Note: For details about these controls, see the section "Adjust Hue and Saturation."

8 Click **OK**.

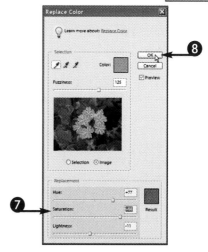

Photoshop Elements replaces the selected color.

How can I replace more than one area of color?

You can press Shift and then click inside your image to add other colors to your selection. If you are viewing the Selection preview, the white area inside the preview box increases as you click. To deselect colors from your selection, press Alt (option) and then click a color inside your image.

Can I replace a color in my image using the painting tools?

Yes. For example, you can click the Paint Bucket tool ( ), select a Foreground color, and replace a color in your image with the selected color. For more on using Photoshop Elements painting tools, see Chapter 10.

Equalize Colors

You can use the Equalize filter to redistribute the brightness values in your image. This can lighten an overly dark or gray photo.

Photoshop Elements equalizes an image by finding the lightest and darkest colors in the image and converting them to white and black. It also redistributes the colors in between.

If you make a selection before performing the command, Elements asks whether you want to equalize only the selection or equalize the entire image based on the selection.

Equalize Colors

① Click **Filter**.

② Click **Adjustments**.

③ Click **Equalize**.

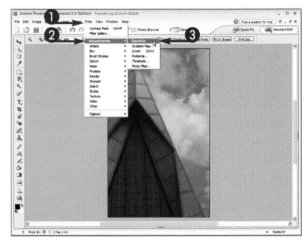

Photoshop Elements equalizes the colors in the image.

Posterize Colors

You can reduce the number of colors in your image using the Posterize filter, which can give a photographic image a solid-color poster look.

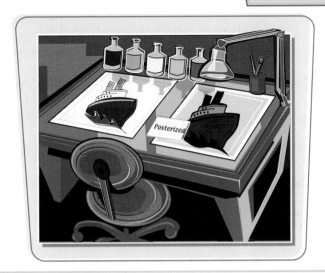

If you make a selection before performing the Posterize command, you only affect the selected pixels. Similarly, if you have a multilayered image, your adjustments only affect the selected layer. See Chapter 4 to make a selection and Chapter 6 for more on layers.

Posterize Colors

① Click **Filter**.

② Click **Adjustments**.

③ Click **Posterize**.

The Posterize dialog box appears.

④ Type the number of levels.

More levels mean more solid colors in the resulting image.

Photoshop Elements posterizes the image.

⑤ Click **OK**.

Photoshop Elements applies the changes.

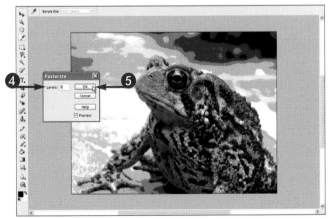

Boost Colors with the Multiply Blending Mode

You can use the Multiply blending mode to strengthen and intensify colors in your photo. For example, if environmental light and chemicals have faded your color Polaroid over time, you can give the image a color boost with the Multiply blending mode. You can control the intensity of the blending mode by setting an opacity level. Professional photographers also use this technique to create an instant color boost in images.

For best results, assign the Multiply blending mode to an Adjustment layer before applying the mode. By duplicating your image and then applying a blending mode, you can stack brightness levels in the image layers to increase color strength. Keep in mind, however, that boosting colors also boosts the darker colors in your image.

Boost Colors with the Multiply Blending Mode

① Duplicate the layer you want to adjust.

● The fastest way to duplicate the layer is to drag and drop the layer over the New Layer button ([⬚]).

Note: See Chapter 6 to read more about layers.

② Click here and then click **Multiply**.

Photoshop Elements applies the Multiply blending mode.

3 Click here and then click and drag the 🔲 that appears to lessen the effect.

● If an area of the layer is too dark, you can click and drag the Eraser tool (🖉) to erase the Multiply mode over an area.

Note: For more about the Eraser tool, see Chapter 10.

In this example, the Eraser tool is applied to the darker pixels here to lighten the area.

TIP

How can I boost an area of pixels rather than an entire layer?

1 Select the pixels using a selection tool.

Note: See Chapter 4 for more on selecting parts of your image.

2 Click **Layer**.

3 Click **New**.

4 Click **Layer via Copy**.

Photoshop Elements copies the selected pixels to a new layer in which you can apply the Multiply blending mode.

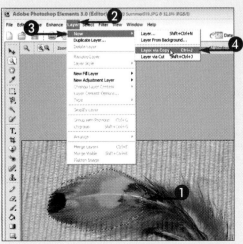

Turn a Color Photo into Black and White

You can change the image mode to turn a color photo into a black and white photo. Elements accomplishes this by converting the colors to grayscale. You may want to make a picture black and white to create a dramatic effect or to publish the photo in a non-color newsletter or brochure.

When you make a color photo into grayscale, the change is permanent. For this reason, you may want to copy the image file before making the change so the original file is still intact with full color. See Chapter 2 to read how to save files.

Turn a Color Photo into Black and White

① Click **Image**.

② Click **Mode**.

③ Click **Grayscale**.

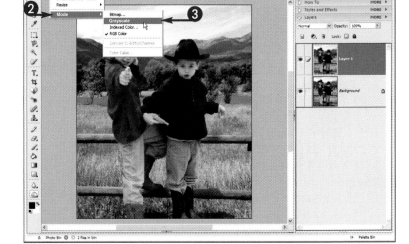

● If your image has multiple layers, you may need to flatten the layers first before proceeding. Click **Flatten**.

Note: For more about flattening images, see Chapter 6.

Photoshop Elements applies the change.

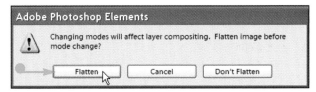

● If your image is one layer, Photoshop Elements displays a prompt box asking if you want to discard color information or not. Click **OK**.

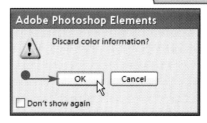

Photoshop Elements applies the change.

TIP

Can I remove color from just one color channel?

Yes. You can leave your image in RGB color mode and just desaturate the color channels using the Hue/Saturation dialog box:

1 Click **Enhance**.

2 Click **Adjust Color**.

3 Click **Hue/Saturation**.

4 In the Hue/Saturation dialog box, click here and then click a color channel.

5 Drag the Saturation □ to the left.

6 Click **OK** to desaturate the color channel.

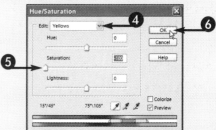

Add Color to a Black and White Photo

You can add color to a black and white photo using any of the painting tools. Adding a little bit of color can really enhance an old black and white image. You must first turn the image into an RGB Color image. Color you add to the photo does not look quite the same as a full color photo; however, you can use bits of color to spruce up the image. For example, you can add color to a baby's cheeks or to articles of clothing.

When you turn a black and white photo into an RGB color photo, the change is permanent. For this reason, you may want to copy the image file before changing image modes so that the original file is still intact in its black and white state. For best results, always perform color changes on duplicate or adjustment layers. See Chapter 2 to read how to save files or see Chapter 6 for more about layers.

① Click **Image**.

② Click **Mode**.

③ Click **RGB Color**.

● If your image has multiple layers, you may need to flatten the layers first before proceeding. In the prompt box that appears, click **Flatten** to continue.

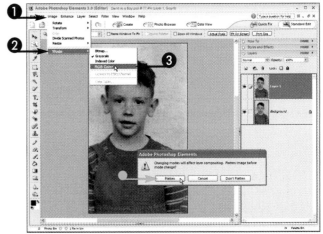

④ Duplicate the Background layer.

Note: See Chapter 6 for more on how to work with layers.

⑤ Click the Brush tool (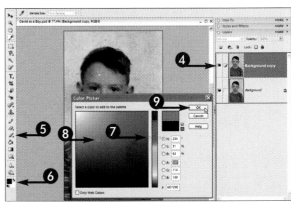).

⑥ Click the Foreground color.

⑦ In the Color Picker dialog box, click a color range.

⑧ Click a color.

⑨ Click **OK**.

🔟 Click and drag to paint the color on the photo.

Photoshop Elements applies the change.

● You can set a lower Opacity level to make the painting effect subtler.

● You can also use the Paint Bucket tool to fill in color in a selected group of pixels in one quick click.

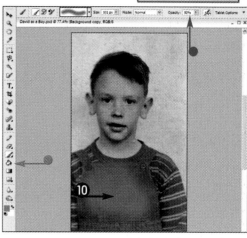

This example shows color added to articles of clothing in the image.

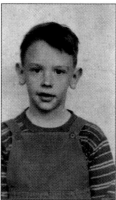

TIP

How do I tone down a layer color?

You can change the layer opacity in the Layers palette to make the color more transparent. Follow these steps:

① Click the layer containing the color you want to edit.

② Click here and then click and drag the ▢ that appears.

Photoshop Elements automatically adjusts the color as you drag.

Note: See Chapter 6 to read more about working with layers.

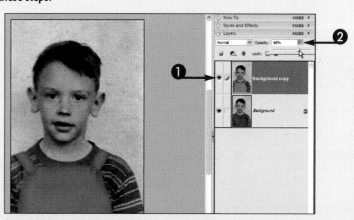

Painting and Drawing on Photos

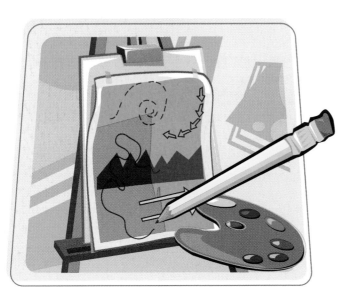

Want to add extra elements to your photos, such as lines, shapes, or solid areas of color? Photoshop Elements offers a variety of tools with which you can use to paint and draw on your images as well as add shapes and colors. This chapter introduces you to a few of those tools and their many uses.

**Set the Foreground and
Background Colors** 180

Add Color with the Brush Tool 182

Change Brush Styles 184

Add Color with the Paint Bucket Tool 186

Draw a Shape 188

Draw a Line 190

Erase an Area 192

Apply a Gradient 194

Set the Foreground and Background Colors

You can select colors to use with many of the painting and drawing tools in Photoshop Elements. For example, you can choose a color to paint on the photo with the Brush tool or draw on the photo with the Pencil tool. You can select two colors to work with at a time — a foreground color and a background color. When you paint with the Brush tool, you apply foreground color. You apply a background color when you use the Eraser tool on the background layer, enlarge the image canvas, or cut pieces out of your image.

See the section "Add Color with the Brush Tool" for more on how to paint on a photo. See the section "Erase an Area" for more on using the Eraser.

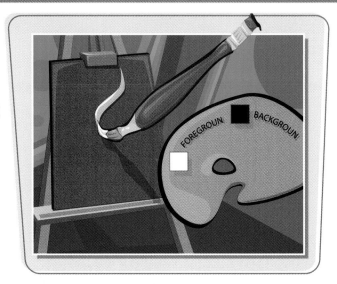

Set the Foreground and Background Colors

SET THE FOREGROUND COLOR

① Click the Foreground Color box (■).

The Color Picker dialog box appears.

② Click and drag ◁ to select a color range.

③ Click a color.

④ Click **OK**.

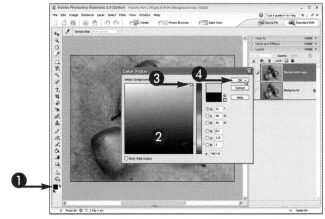

● The selected color appears in the Foreground Color box.

● When you apply a tool that uses a foreground color, Photoshop Elements paints or draws the foreground color on the photo.

This example uses the Brush tool.

Note: For more on painting tools, see the section "Add Color with the Brush Tool."

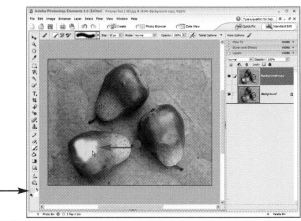

SET THE BACKGROUND COLOR

1 Click the Background Color box (■).

The Color Picker dialog box appears.

2 Click and drag ◁ to select a color range.

3 Click a color.

4 Click **OK**.

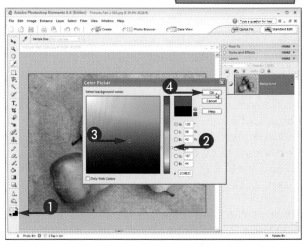

● When you apply a tool that uses a background color, such as the Eraser tool, Photoshop Elements applies the background color.

Erasing occurs only in the background layer; in other layers, the eraser turns pixels transparent.

Note: See Chapter 6 for a full discussion of layers.

TIPS

How do I reset the foreground and background colors?

Click the Default button (■) to the lower-left of the Foreground and Background icons. Doing so resets the colors to black and white. You can also click the Switch icon (↺) to swap the foreground and background colors.

Does Photoshop Elements offer a set of common colors?

Yes. You can select a color to paint or draw on your photo from the Swatches palette, which includes a set of commonly used colors. To view the palette, click **Window** and then **Color Swatches**. You can click the color you want to use, and the Foreground color box on the toolbox immediately reflects your choice.

Add Color with the Brush Tool

You can use the Brush tool to add color to your image. You may find the paintbrush useful for applying bands of color or small patches of color. You can use the tool to cover unwanted elements or change the appearance of clothing or a backdrop. When applying the Brush tool, you can control the size of the brushstrokes by choosing a brush size. For realistic results, turn on the Airbrush feature to apply a softer line of color.

To limit where the brush applies color, create a selection before using the tool. For details, see Chapter 4.

Add Color with the Brush Tool

① Click the Brush tool (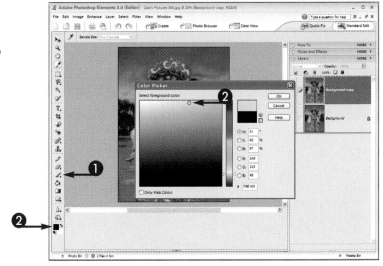).

② Click ■ to select a color with which to paint.

Note: For details, see the section "Select the Foreground and Background Colors."

③ Click here and then click a brush size and type.

● You can also click here and adjust the slider to set a brush size.

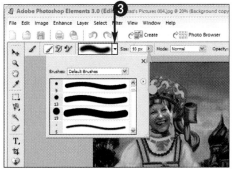

Click the Airbrush feature ().

The Airbrush feature paints with soft edges, like a real airbrush, for better touch-up effects.

● You can click here to adjust the slider to change the opacity of the paint effect.

❺ Click and drag ○ on the image.

Photoshop Elements applies color per your specifications.

The more you click and drag ○, the more color appears.

● To undo the most recent brush stroke, you can click **Edit** and then **Undo Brush Tool** or click the Undo button (⟲).

TIPS

How do I paint thin lines?

Use the Pencil tool (✎), which is similar to the Brush tool (✎) except that it paints only thin, hard-edged lines. Like the Paintbrush, the Pencil applies the foreground color. See the section "Draw a Line" for more on using the Pencil tool.

What can I do with the Impressionist Brush tool?

You can apply artistic styles to your image with the Impressionist Brush. The brush creates its effect by blending existing colors in an image together. The Impressionist Brush does not add any foreground or background color to your image.

Change Brush Styles

Many of the Photoshop Elements tools, such as the Brush tool, involve using a brush to paint on color and other special effects. You can select from a variety of predefined brush styles to apply color in different ways. You can also create a custom brush style. Photoshop Elements displays a set of default brush styles, or you can choose another set from a list of preset brush styles.

Change Brush Styles

SELECT FROM A PREDEFINED SET

1 Click .

2 Click the Brush ▾.

3 Click here and then click a set of brushes.

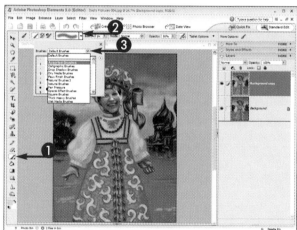

The set appears in the brush menu.

4 Click a brush style to select it.

● The cursor changes to the new brush shape.

Note: To apply the brush, see the section "Add Color with the Brush Tool."

CUSTOMIZE A BRUSH

1 Click the **More Options** button.

A palette of brush options appears.

2 Click and drag the sliders (⬜) or type values to define the new brush attributes.

● To save the new settings, you can click this option (⬜ changes to ☑).

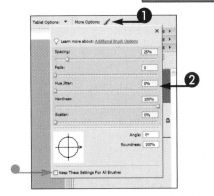

● The brush style appears in the brush menu.

3 Click and drag the brush on the photo.

The new attributes are applied to the area.

Note: *To apply the brush, see the section "Add Color with the Brush Tool."*

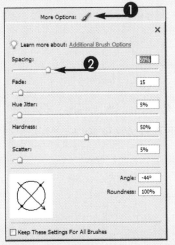

TIP

How can I make a brush apply dots instead of a line?

1 Click the **More Options** button to open the More Options settings in the Options bar.

2 Click and drag ⬜ to increase the Spacing value to greater than 100%.

3 When you click and drag your cursor, you get a discontiguous brush stroke.

Add Color with the Paint Bucket Tool

You can fill areas in your image with solid color using the Paint Bucket tool. You can use this technique to change the color of clothes, eyes, the sky, backgrounds, and more. When you apply the Paint Bucket tool, it affects adjacent pixels in the image. You can set the Paint Bucket's Tolerance value to determine what range of colors the paint bucket affects in the image when you apply it.

Add Color with the Paint Bucket Tool

SELECT THE PAINT BUCKET TOOL

① Click the Paint Bucket tool (⬛).

② Click ⬛ to select a color for painting.

Note: For details, see the section "Select the Foreground and Background Colors."

SET THE TOLERANCE

③ Type a Tolerance value from 0 to 255.

④ Click inside the image.

Photoshop Elements fills an area of the image with the foreground color.

SET IMAGE OPACITY

5 To fill an area with a semitransparent color, type a percentage value of less than 100% in the Opacity field.

6 Click inside the image.

Photoshop Elements fills an area with see-through paint.

FILL NONCONTIGUOUS AREAS

7 To fill non-contiguous similar areas throughout the image, click the **Contiguous** option (☑ changes to ☐).

8 Click inside the selection.

Photoshop Elements fills similar areas of the image, even if they are not contiguous with the clicked pixel.

TIPS

How can I reset a tool to the default settings?
Click the tool's icon on the far-left side of the Options bar and select **Reset Tools** from the menu that appears. This resets the opacity to 100%, the blending mode to Normal, and other attributes to their startup values. You can also click **Reset All Tools** from the menu to reset all the Elements tools to their default settings.

How do I fill a selection or an entire layer?
You can use the Fill command to fill a selection or a layer with a solid or semitransparent color. Filling is an easy way to change the color of an object in your image. To activate the command, click **Edit** and then **Fill Selection**. This opens the Fill Layer dialog box, which you can use to select what you want to fill and set an opacity for the fill color.

You can create solid shapes in your image using Photoshop Elements' many shape tools. Shapes offer an easy way to add whimsical objects, labels, or buttons to an image.

When you add a shape to an image, Elements places the shape in its own layer. This makes it easy to move and transform the shape later on. For more information about layers, see Chapter 6.

Draw a Shape

① Click the Custom Shape tool (▢).

The Custom Shape tool shares space on the toolbox with the other shape tools.

Note: See Chapter 1 for more about working with toolbox tools.

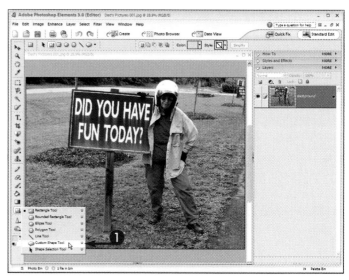

You can select from standard shapes in the Options bar.

② Click here and then click a shape.

③ Press Enter (Return) to close the menu.

④ Click here and then click a style for your shape.

Photoshop Elements offers a variety of 3D styles.

⑤ Press **Enter** (**Return**) to close the menu.

● You can click the Color box ( ) to select a different shape fill color.

⑥ Click and drag your cursor (＋) to draw the shape.

● Photoshop Elements places the shape in its own layer.

Note: For more about layers, see Chapter 6.

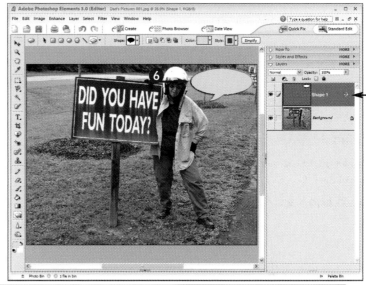

TIP

How do I resize a shape after I draw it?

① Click the shape's layer.

② Click the Custom Shape tool ( ).

③ Click **Image**.

④ Click **Transform Shape**.

⑤ Click a transform command.

You can then resize the shape just like you would a selection.

Note: See Chapter 5 for more details on transformations.

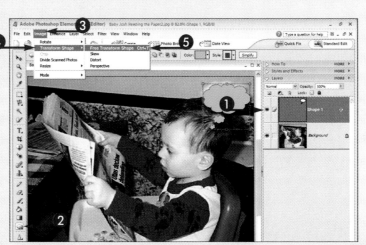

You can draw all kinds of lines on your photo using several different tools. You can draw a straight line with an arrow using Photoshop Elements' Custom Shape tool. You can customize the line with arrows, giving you an easy way to point out elements in your image. You can also draw free-form lines with the Pencil tool.

When you add a line to an image with the Line tool, Elements places the line in its own layer. This makes it easy to move and transform the line later on. For more information about layers, see Chapter 6.

Draw a Line

DRAW A LINE WITH THE LINE TOOL

1 Click the Line tool (▱).

The Line tool shares space on the toolbox with the other shape tools.

2 Click here and then click **Start** or **End** to include arrowheads on your line (☐ changes to ☑).

● You can also specify the shape of the arrowheads by typing values here.

3 Press (Enter) ((Return)).

4 Type a line weight.

5 Click ☐ to select a different line color.

● You can click here to set a style for your line.

6 Press (Enter) ((Return)) to close the menu.

7 Click and drag your cursor (+) to draw the line.

DRAW A LINE WITH THE PENCIL TOOL

1 Click the Pencil tool (✎).

2 Click here and then click a line brush shape or style.

● You can also set a line width here.

3 Click and drag to draw a free-form line.

Photoshop Elements draws a line on the image.

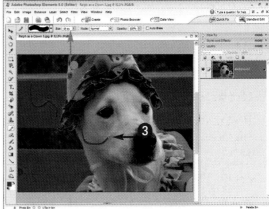

TIP

Can I add a line to a selected object in my photo?

You can add a line, called a *stroke* in Elements, to a selected area of your image. For example, you can add an outline around the subject of a photo. Strokes help you highlight objects in your images. You can set the outline inside the selection border, outside the selection border, or on the selection border. To add a stroke, follow these steps:

1 Select the area you want to outline.

2 Click **Edit**.

3 Click **Stroke (Outline) Selection**.

The Stroke dialog box opens.

4 Type a width for the line.

● You can click here to select a color for the line.

5 Click a location.

6 Click **OK**.

● Photoshop Elements applies the stroke.

Erase an Area

You can use the Eraser tool to erase portions of your photo. For example, you may want to erase an unwanted object. When you apply the Eraser tool on the background layer, the erased pixels are replaced with the selected background color. When you erase in other layers, the eraser turns the pixels transparent, revealing any underlying layers.

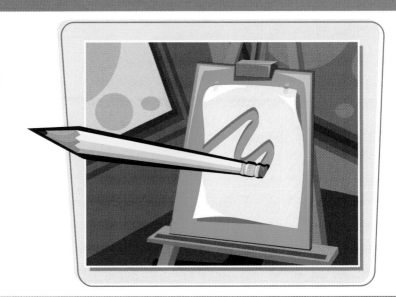

Erase an Area

1 Click the Eraser tool (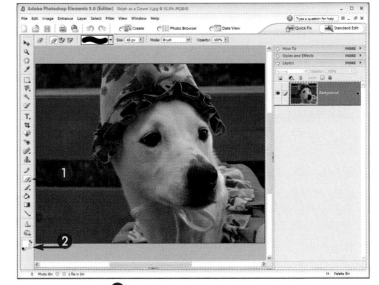).

2 Click ■ to select a color to appear in place of the erased pixels.

Note: For details, see the section "Select the Foreground and Background Colors."

3 Click here and then click an eraser size and type.

● You can also click here and adjust the slider to set an eraser size.

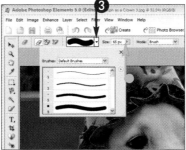

4 Click and drag your cursor (◯) to erase on the image.

In this example, portions of the background layer are erased and replaced with the background color.

In this example, portions of a layer are erased to reveal the underlying layer.

What do the other eraser types do?

You can use the Background Eraser tool (🖼) to sample the color and erase only the same color pixels you drag over in your image. The Magic Eraser tool (🖼) changes all the adjacent similar pixels with a click. You can click either tool in the Options bar after clicking the Eraser tool.

Which eraser mode should I use?

You can choose from three different eraser modes: Brush, Pencil, and Block. To change to a different mode, click the Mode arrow on the Options bar and then select a mode. **Brush** mode, which is the default mode, enables you to move your eraser over the image like a paintbrush. The **Pencil** mode acts like a pencil while erasing. The **Block** mode turns the eraser cursor into a block shape for erasing.

You can apply a gradient, which is a blend from one color to another. This gives objects in your image a radiant or 3D look. You can apply a gradient to a selected portion of an image.

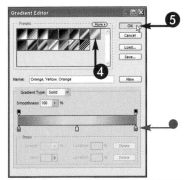

Apply a Gradient

1 Make a selection.

Note: See Chapter 4 for more on making selections.

2 Click the Gradient tool (▣).

A linear gradient is the default. You can select different geometries in the Options bar.

3 Click the gradient swatch.

The Gradient Editor opens.

4 Click a preset gradient type from the top box

● You can define a custom gradient by using these settings.

5 Click **OK**.

6 Click and drag your cursor ($+$) inside the selection.

This defines the direction and transition of the gradient.

Dragging a long line with the tool produces a gradual transition.

Dragging a short line with the tool produces an abrupt transition.

Photoshop Elements generates a gradient inside the selection.

How can I highlight an object in my image using a gradient?

1 Place the object in its own layer.

2 Create a new layer below the object where you can create the gradient.

Note: For more information about layers, see Chapter 6.

3 Click 🔲.

4 Click the Radial Gradient button (🔲).

5 Click and drag your cursor ($+$) to create the gradient.

This highlights the object with a burst of color.

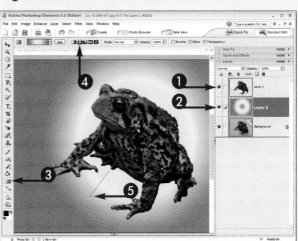

Applying Filters

With Photoshop Elements' filters, you can quickly and easily apply enhancements to your image, including artistic effects, texture effects, and distortions. Filters can help you correct defects in your images or let you turn a photograph into something resembling an impressionist painting. Photoshop Elements comes with over 100 filters. But this chapter highlights only a few. For details about all the filters, see the Help documentation.

Blur an Image...198

Distort an Image 200

Turn an Image into a Painting 202

Turn an Image into a Sketch 204

Add Noise to an Image 206

Pixelate an Image 208

Emboss an Image 210

Blur an Image

You can use the Blur filters to create a variety of blurring effects in your photos. For example, you can use a Gaussian Blur filter to obscure background objects while keeping foreground objects in focus. By diminishing a busy background, for example, you can make the image look as if it has a short depth of field. A short depth of field keeps the foreground subject in focus while the background is out of focus.

You might blur away a background to eliminate unwanted clutter behind the subject, or to emphasize the subject of your photo. You can also use the technique in an artistic way to blur away people surrounding your subject.

Blur an Image

① Select the layer to which you want to apply the filter.

Note: For more about layers, see Chapter 6.

Note: To apply the filter to just part of your image, you can make the selection with a selection tool. For more on selection tools, see Chapter 4.

② Click **Filter**.

③ Click **Blur**.

④ Click **Gaussian Blur**.

The Gaussian Blur dialog box appears.

● A small preview area displays a preview of the filter's effect.

⑤ Click ▢ or ⊞ to zoom out or in.

⑥ Click the **Preview** option to preview the effect in the main window (▢ changes to ☑).

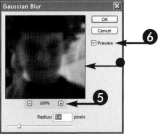

7 Click and drag the Radius slider () to control the amount of blur added.

In this example, boosting the Radius value increased the amount of blur.

8 Click **OK**.

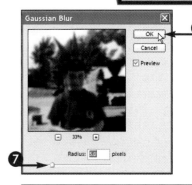

Photoshop Elements applies the filter.

In this example, the background layer is blurred while the foreground remains unchanged.

Experiment with the other Blur filters to create other kinds of blurring effects in your image.

Note: For more on sharpening an image with a filter, see Chapter 7.

TIP

How do I add directional blurring to an image?

1 Select the object to blur.

2 Click **Filter**.

3 Click **Blur**.

4 Click **Motion Blur**.

5 In the Motion Blur dialog box click and drag the Angle dial to define the direction of the blur.

6 Click and drag to adjust the amount of blur.

7 Click **OK** to apply the filter.

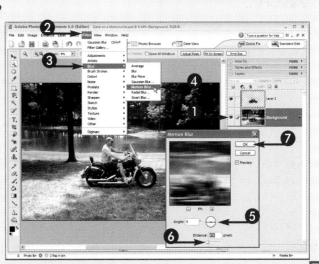

Distort an Image

You can use any of the Distort filters to stretch and squeeze your image to create the appearance of waves, glass, swirls, and more. For example, the Twirl filter turns the image into a swirl of colors and the Liquify filter makes parts of the image seem to drip. Each Distort filter comes with its own unique set of controls for adjusting the effect.

To apply the filter to just part of your image, make the selection with a selection tool. See Chapter 4 to use the selection tools.

Distort an Image

① Select the layer to which you want to apply the filter.

Note: For more about layers, see Chapter 6.

② Click **Filter**.

③ Click **Distort**.

④ Click an effect.

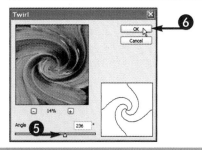

The filter's associated dialog box appears.

⑤ Make adjustments to the filter's settings to fine-tune the effect.

With some filters, you can preview the effect before assigning it to the image.

⑥ Click **OK**.

Photoshop Elements applies the filter.

In this example, the Twirl distortion filter is applied.

In this example, the Zig Zag distortion filter is applied.

Note: You can use the other types of filters available in the Filters menu to create different kinds of special effects in your photos.

 TIPS

How many filters does Photoshop Elements offer?

Photoshop Elements has 108 filters grouped into 14 different categories. Mac users have 12 categories. You can experiment with each one to find out what sort of effects they have on your image. Some of the more popular filters include the **Unsharp Mask**, used for sharpening an image's focus, and the **Lighting Effects** filter, which enables you to create the illusion of spot lights and other specialized lights in your photos. See Chapter 7 and 8 for more on using these two types of filters.

Is there another way to distort a selection?

Yes. You can use the Distort command to distort a selected element in your photo. First select the element, click **Image**, click **Transform**, and then click **Distort**. Photoshop Elements surrounds the selection with handles, which you can then drag to distort the element.

Turn an Image into a Painting

You can use many of Photoshop Elements' Artistic filters to make your image look as if you created it with a paintbrush or other art media. The Dry Brush filter, for example, applies a painted effect by converting similarly colored areas in your image to solid colors.

To apply the filter to just part of your image, you can make the selection with a selection tool. See Chapter 4 to use selection tools.

Turn an Image into a Painting

① Select the layer to which you want to apply the filter.

Note: *For more about layers, see Chapter 6.*

In this example, the image has a single background layer.

② Click **Filter**.

③ Click **Artistic**.

④ Click an effect.

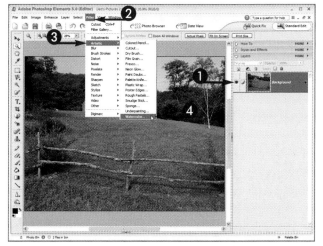

The Filter Gallery dialog box appears.

⑤ Make adjustments to the filter's settings to fine-tune the effect.

● With some filters, you can preview the effect before assigning it to the image. Click ⊟ or ⊞ to zoom out or in.

⑥ Click **OK**.

Photoshop Elements applies the filter.

In this example, the Watercolor filter is applied.

In this example, the Cutout filter is applied.

You can use the other types of filters available in the Filters menu to create different kinds of special effects in your photos.

TIP

How do I make my image look like a sponge painting?

You can use the Sponge filter to reduce details and modify the image's shapes:

① Follow steps **1** to **4** in this section, but select **Sponge** in step **4**.

② In the Sponge dialog box, click and drag ▢ to define the size and contrast of the sponge strokes.

③ Click **OK**.

Photoshop Elements applies the filter.

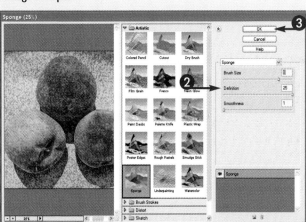

Turn an Image into a Sketch

The Sketch filters add outlining effects to your image. The Charcoal filter, for example, makes an image look as if you sketched it using charcoal on paper.

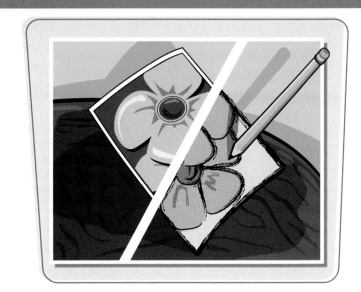

You use the foreground as the charcoal color and the background as the paper color. Changing these alters the filter's effect. See Chapter 9 to adjust color.

To apply the filter to just part of your image, you can make the selection with a selection tool. To use the selection tools, see Chapter 4.

Turn an Image into a Sketch

① Select the layer to which you want to apply the filter.

Note: For more about layers, see Chapter 6.

In this example, the image has a single background layer.

② Click **Filter**.

③ Click **Sketch**.

④ Click **Charcoal**.

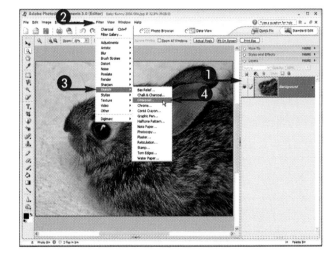

The Charcoal dialog box appears.

A window displays a preview of the filter's effect.

⑤ Click 🔲 or ⊞ to zoom out or in.

⑥ Click and drag the sliders (🔲) to control the filter's effect.

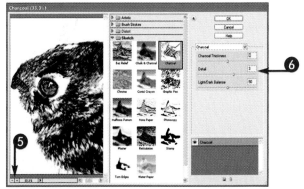

In this example, the thickness of the charcoal strokes is increased.

The Light/Dark Balance setting is also increased to darken the image.

7 Click **OK**.

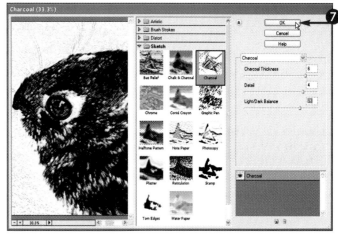

Photoshop Elements applies the filter.

TIP

What does the Photocopy filter do?

The Photocopy filter converts your image's shadows and midtones to the foreground color and highlights to the background color to make the image look like a photocopy:

1 Follow steps **1** to **4** in this section, selecting **Photocopy** for step **4**.

2 In the Photocopy dialog box, click and drag 🔲 to control the detail and darkness of the colors.

3 Click **OK**.

Photoshop Elements applies the filter.

Add Noise to an Image

Filters in the Noise menu add or remove graininess in your image. You can add graininess with the Add Noise filter.

To apply the filter to just part of your image, you can make the selection with a selection tool. To use the selection tools, see Chapter 4.

Add Noise to an Image

① Select the layer to which you want to apply the filter.

Note: For more about layers, see Chapter 6.

In this example, the image has a single background layer.

② Click **Filter**.

③ Click **Noise**.

④ Click **Add Noise**.

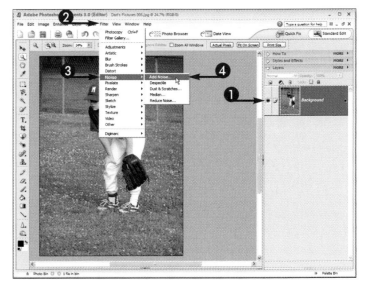

The Add Noise dialog box appears displaying a preview.

⑤ Click ⊟ or ⊞ to zoom out or in.

⑥ Click the **Preview** button to preview the effect in the main window (☐ changes to ☑).

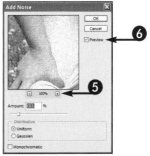

7 Click and drag the Amount slider (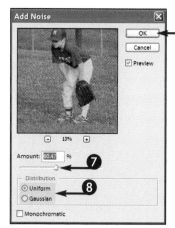) to change the noise.

8 Click here to select how you want the noise distributed (○ changes to ⊙).

Uniform spreads the noise more evenly than Gaussian.

In this example, the Amount value is increased.

9 Click **OK**.

Photoshop Elements applies the filter.

What does the Monochromatic setting in the Add Noise dialog box do?

If you click **Monochromatic** (☐ changes to ☑), Elements adds noise by lightening or darkening pixels in your image. Pixel hues stay the same. At high settings with the Monochromatic setting on, the filter produces a television-static effect.

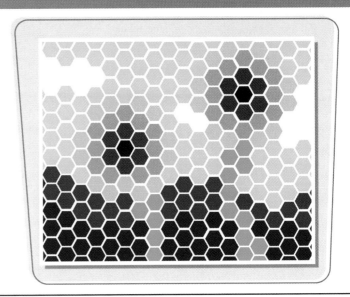

The Pixelate filters divide areas of your image into solid-colored dots or shapes. The Crystallize filter, one example of a Pixelate filter, re-creates your image using colored polygons.

To apply the filter to just part of your image, you can make the selection with a selection tool. To use the selection tools, see Chapter 4.

Pixelate an Image

① Select the layer to which you want to apply the filter.

Note: For more about layers, see Chapter 6.

In this example, the image has a single background layer.

② Click **Filter**.

③ Click **Pixelate**.

④ Click **Crystallize**.

The Crystallize dialog box appears displaying a preview of the filter's effect.

⑤ Click ⊟ or ⊞ to zoom out or in.

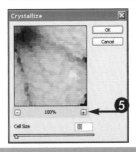

6 Click and drag the Cell Size slider (🔲) to adjust the size of the shapes.

The size can range from 3 to 300.

In this example, the Cell Size has been slightly increased.

7 Click **OK**.

Photoshop Elements applies the filter.

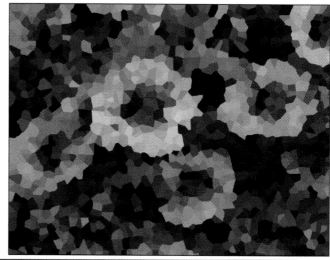

What does the Mosaic filter do?

The Mosaic filter converts your image to a set of solid-color squares. You can control the size of the squares in the filter's dialog box. To apply the filter:

1 Click **Filter**.

2 Click **Pixelate**.

3 Click **Mosaic**.

The Mosaic dialog box opens.

4 Click and drag 🔲 to specify the mosaic square size.

5 Click **OK** to apply the filter.

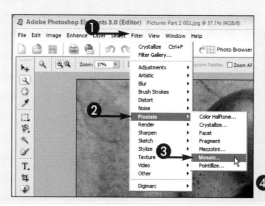

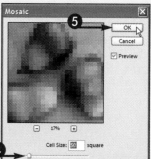

Emboss an Image

You can achieve the effect of a three-dimensional shape pressed into paper with the Emboss filter. You may find this filter useful for generating textured backgrounds.

To apply the filter to just part of your image, you can make the selection with a selection tool. To use the selection tools, see Chapter 4.

Emboss an Image

1 Select the layer to which you want to apply the filter.

Note: For more about layers, see Chapter 6.

In this example, the image has a single background layer.

2 Click **Filter**.

3 Click **Stylize**.

4 Click **Emboss**.

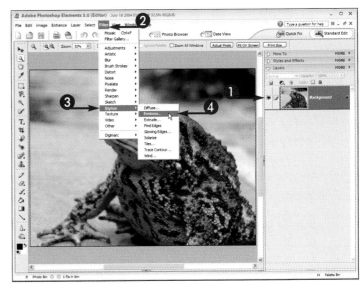

The Emboss dialog box appears.

Photoshop Elements displays a small preview of the effect.

5 Click ⊟ or ⊞ to zoom out or in.

6 Type an angle to specify in which direction to shadow the image.

● You can also click and drag the angle dial to set an angle.

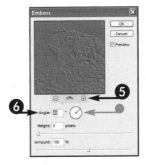

7 Click and drag the Height 🔲 to the desired pixel height.

You can specify a height from 1 to 10 to set the strength of the embossing.

8 Click and drag the Amount 🔲 to set the amount of embossing detail.

You can specify an amount from 1 to 500 to set the number of edges the filter affects.

9 Click **OK**.

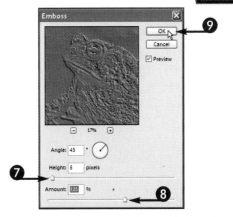

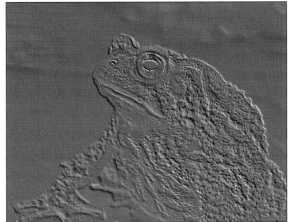

Do I have another way to create an embossed effect in an image?

Yes. You can use the Bas Relief filter to get a similar effect. It creates a two-toned embossed effect by reducing an image to the current foreground and background colors. To apply the filter:

1 Follow steps **1** to **4** in this section, clicking **Sketch** in step **3** and **Bas Relief** in step **4**.

2 In the Bas Relief dialog box, click and drag 🔲 to control the detail.

3 Click and drag 🔲 to control the smoothness.

4 Click **OK**.

Photoshop Elements applies the filter.

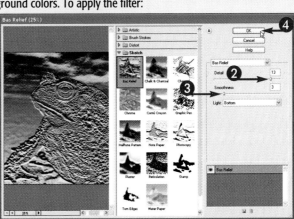

Adding Text Elements

Do you want to add letters and words to your photos and illustrations? Photoshop Elements lets you add text to your images and precisely control the appearance and layout of the text. You can also stylize your text using Elements' filters and other tools.

Add Text **214**

Change the Formatting of Text **216**

Change the Color of Text **218**

Apply a Filter to Text **220**

Create Warped Text **222**

Create Outlined Text **224**

Add a Drop Shadow to Text **225**

Adding text enables you to label elements in your image or use letters and words in artistic ways. When you add text, it appears in its own layer. You can manipulate text layers in your image to move or stylize the text.

Add Text

① Click the Type tool (T).

② Click where you want the new text to begin.

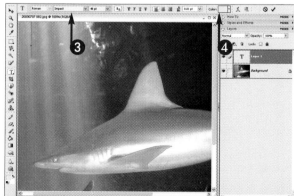

③ Click here and then select a style, font, and size for your text.

④ Click the Color box (▭) to select a color for your text.

⑤ Type your text.

To create a line break, press **Enter** (**Return** on a Mac).

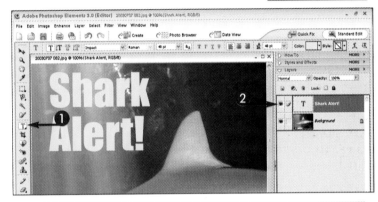

⑥ When you finish typing your text, click ✔ or press **Enter** on your keyboard's number pad.

● You can click ⊘ or press **Esc** to cancel.

● Photoshop Elements places the text in its own layer.

TIPS

How do I reposition my text?

You can move the layer that contains the text with the Move tool (⊹). Click the layer of text, click ⊹, and then click and drag to reposition your text. For more on moving a layer, see Chapter 6.

How do I change the orientation of my text?

Select a text layer and then click the Change the text orientation button (⊤). This converts horizontal text to vertical text. Clicking the button again changes the text back to a horizontal orientation.

Change the Formatting of Text

You can change the font, style, size, and other characteristics of your text. This can help emphasize or de-emphasize your text.

① Click [T].

② Click the text layer that you want to edit.

Note: If the Layers palette is not visible, see Chapter 1 to open it.

③ Click and drag to select some text from the selected layer.

● You can double-click the layer thumbnail to select all the text.

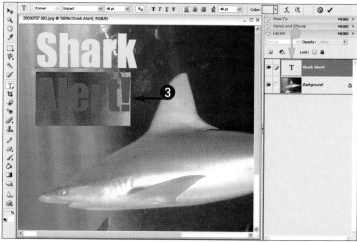

216

④ Click here and select the text's style.

⑤ Click here and select a font.

⑥ Click here and select the text's size.

⑦ Click the Anti-Aliased button ( ) to control the text's antialiasing.

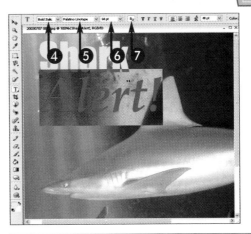

⑧ When you finish formatting your text, click ✓ or press **Enter** on your keyboard's number pad.

● You can click Ⓞ or press **Esc** to cancel.

Photoshop Elements applies the formatting to your text.

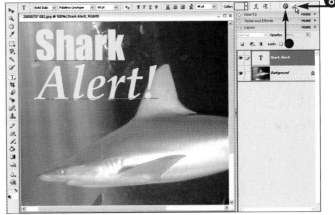

TIPS

What is antialiasing?
Antialiasing is the process of adding semitransparent pixels to curved edges in digital images to make the edges appear smoother. You can apply antialiasing to text to improve its appearance. Text that you do not antialias can sometimes look jagged. You can control the presence and style of your text's antialiasing with the Options bar.

How do I change the alignment of my text?
When creating your text, click one of the three alignment buttons: Left align text ( ), Center text ( ), or Right align text ( ). You may find these options useful when you create multiline passages of text.

Change the Color of Text

You can change the color of your text to make it blend or contrast with the rest of the image. You can change the color of all or just a part of your text.

1 Click 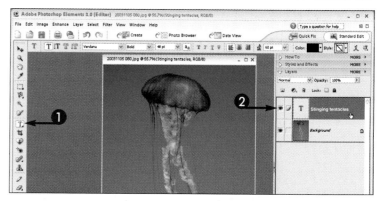.

2 Click the text layer that you want to edit.

Note: If the Layers palette is not visible, see Chapter 1 to open it.

3 Click and drag to select some text.

● You can double-click the layer thumbnail to select all the text.

④ Click here and click a color.

When you place your cursor (🖑) over a color, the 🖑 changes to an eyedropper (✐).

⑤ Press **Enter** on your keyboard's number pad.

⑥ Click ✔ or press **Enter** on your keyboard's number pad again.

● You can click ⊘ or press **Esc** to cancel.

Photoshop Elements changes the text to the new color.

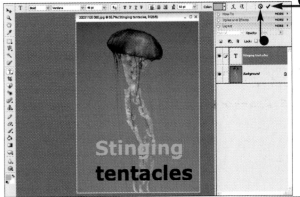

TIP

How do I change type color using the Swatches palette?

The Swatches palette offers an alternative to the color menu when selecting colors:

① Click the text layer in the Layers palette.

② Click and drag in the image window to select the text you want to recolor.

③ Click a color in the Swatches palette.

Note: See Chapter 1 to read how to open the Layer and Swatches palettes.

The text changes color.

● To see the actual new color, click away from the type in the image window to deselect it.

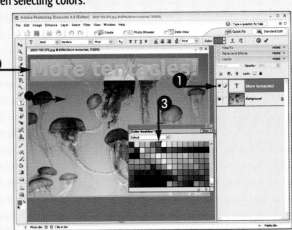

Apply a Filter to Text

You can add interesting effects to your text with Elements' filters. To apply a filter to text, you must first simplify it. *Simplifying* converts your type layer into a regular Elements layer. You can no longer edit simplified text using the text tools.

For more about filters, see Chapter 11.

① Select the text layer to which you want to apply a filter.

Note: *If the Layers palette is not visible, see Chapter 1 to open it.*

② Click **Filter**.

③ Click a filter submenu.

④ Click a filter.

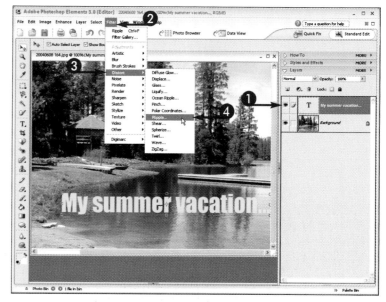

A dialog box appears asking if you want to simplify the layer.

⑤ Click **OK**.

● Photoshop Elements converts the text layer to a regular layer.

To keep a copy of your editable text layer, you can duplicate it before applying the filter. See Chapter 6 for details.

⑥ Specify your filter settings.

Note: For more information on filter settings, see Chapter 11.

⑦ Click **OK**.

Photoshop Elements applies the filter to the text.

This example adds a distortion effect to the text with the Ripple filter.

TIPS

How can I create semitransparent text?

Select the text layer in the Layers palette and then reduce the layer's opacity to less than 100%. This makes the type semitransparent. For details about changing opacity, see Chapter 6.

How can I turn my text into neon letters?

You can apply the Neon Glow filter to your text. You can locate this filter under the Artistic submenu.

Create Warped Text

Elements' Warp feature lets you easily bend and distort layers of text. This can help you stylize your text to match the theme of your image.

1 Click .

2 Click the text layer that you want to warp.

Note: If the Layers palette is not visible, see Chapter 1 to open it.

3 Click the Create Warped Text button (⌐).

The Warp Text dialog box appears.

4 Click here and then click a warp style.

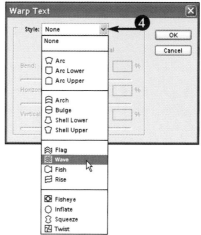

⑤ Click an orientation for the warp effect (◯ changes to ◉).

⑥ Adjust the Bend and Distortion values by clicking and dragging the sliders (▢).

The Bend and Distortion values determine how Elements affects the warp.

For all settings, a value of 0% means Elements does not apply a warp.

⑦ Click **OK**.

Photoshop Elements warps the text.

You can still edit the format, color, and other characteristics of the type when you apply warp.

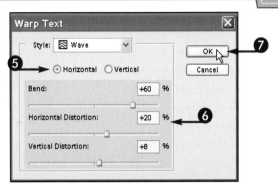

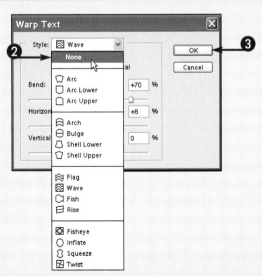

TIP

How do I unwarp text?

❶ Follow steps **1** to **3** in this section.

❷ In the Warp dialog box, click ☑ (▣ on a Mac) and select **None**.

❸ Click **OK**.

Your text unwarps.

Create Outlined Text

You can create outlined text to make letters and words in your images stand out.

Outlined text is a type of effect. For more information about Elements' effects, see Chapter 13.

Outlined text is a type of effect. For more information about Elements' effects, see Chapter 13.

Create Outlined Text

① In the Layers palette, click the text layer that you want to outline.

② Open the Styles and Effects palette.

Note: If the Layers and Styles and Effects palettes are not visible, see Chapter 1 to open them.

③ Click here and then click **Effects**.

Photoshop Elements displays the available effects.

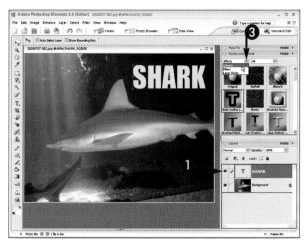

④ Click here and then click **Text Effects**.

Photoshop Elements displays the effects specific to text.

⑤ Double-click an outline effect – **Thin Outline**, **Medium Outline**, or **Bold Outline**.

Photoshop Elements applies the effect to the text.

Add a Drop Shadow to Text

You can cast a shadow next to your text to give the text a 3D look.

Cast Shadow is a type of effect. For more information about Elements' effects, see Chapter 13.

Add a Drop Shadow to Text

① In the Layers palette, click the text layer to which you want to add a drop shadow.

② Open the Styles and Effects palette.

Note: If the Layers and Styles and Effects palettes are not visible, see Chapter 1 to open them.

③ Click here and then click **Effects**.

Photoshop Elements displays the available effects.

④ Click here and then click **Text Effects**.

Photoshop Elements displays the effects specific to text.

⑤ Double-click **Cast Shadow**.

Photoshop Elements applies the effect to the text.

CHAPTER 13

Applying Styles and Effects

You can create special effects for your images by applying Photoshop Elements' built-in styles and effects. The effects let you add shadows, glows, and 3D appearances to your art. You can also add special effects to your layers with Elements' layer styles.

Add a Drop Shadow to a Photo......................228

Add a Drop Shadow to a Layer 230

Frame an Image..232

Add a Fancy Background...............................234

Add Beveling to a Layer................................236

Add an Outer Glow to a Layer 238

Add a Fancy Covering to a Layer..................240

Add a Drop Shadow to a Photo

You can apply a drop shadow to make your photo look like it floats above the image canvas.

You can also apply a drop shadow to just a layer. See the section "Add a Drop Shadow to a Layer" for more information.

Because this effect flattens the layers in your multilayer image, it is best to apply it last.

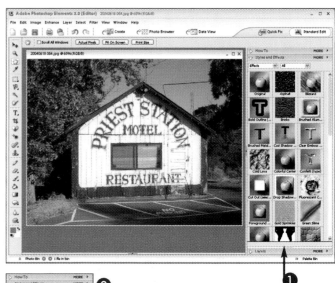

Add a Drop Shadow to a Photo

1 Open the Styles and Effects palette.

Note: For more information on opening and using palettes, see Chapter 1.

2 Click here and then click **Frames**.

The frame effects appear.

③ Double-click The **Drop Shadow Frame** effect.

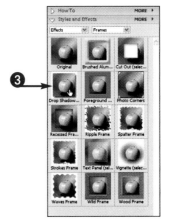

Photoshop Elements increases the canvas size and places an offset shadow under the image.

TIPS

What other shadow effects are there?

You can make a selection to your image and then apply the **Recessed Frame** effect. This places a shadow along the inner edge of the selection, creating an effect that is opposite of a drop shadow effect.

How do I undo an effect?

Immediately after applying the effect, you can click **Edit** and then **Undo**. You can also undo an effect by using the Undo History palette. Click **Window** and then **Undo History** to access it.

Add a Drop Shadow to a Layer

You can add a drop shadow to a layer to give objects in your photo a 3D look.

① Open the Layers palette.

② Open the Styles and Effects palette.

Note: For more information on opening and using palettes, see Chapter 1.

③ Click the layer to which you want to add a drop shadow.

④ Click here and then and click **Layer Styles**.

⑤ Click here and then click **Drop Shadows**.

The drop shadow styles display.

6 Click a drop shadow style.

Photoshop Elements applies the drop shadow to the layer.

7 Double-click the Style icon () in the affected layer.

The Style Settings dialog box opens.

8 Click and drag the **Lighting Angle** dial to specify the direction of the shadowing.

9 Click and drag the Shadow Distance 🔲 to increase or decrease the distance of the shadow from your layer.

10 Click **OK**.

Photoshop Elements applies the style settings.

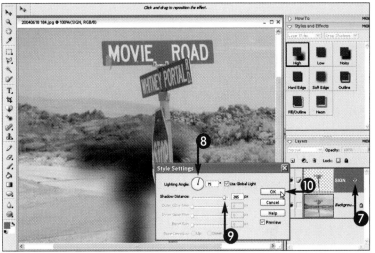

TIP

How do I add an inner shadow to a layer?

An inner shadow creates a "cut out" effect, with the selected layer appearing to drop behind the image canvas. This can have an interesting effect when applied to a layer of text. See Chapter 12 for more about text. To add this effect:

1 Click a layer.

2 Open the Styles and Effects palette.

Note: For more information on opening and using palettes, see Chapter 1.

3 Click here and then click **Layer Styles**.

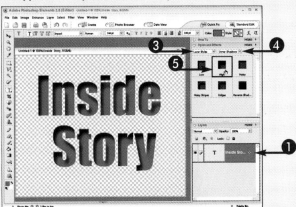

4 Click here and then click **Inner Shadows**.

5 Click an Inner Shadow style.

Photoshop Elements applies the inner shadow.

Frame
an Image

You can apply one of several frame styles to add a traditional or flashy frame around your image.

Because this effect flattens the layers in your image, applying it last is best.

Frame an Image

❶ Open the Styles and Effects palette.

Note: For more information on opening and using palettes, see Chapter 1.

❷ Click here and then click **Frames**.

The frame effects appear.

❸ Double-click an effect.

● You can scroll down to view other effects in the palette.

If you have a multilayered image, a dialog box appears asking if you want to flatten the layers.

④ Click **OK**.

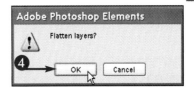

Photoshop Elements creates a frame around the outer edge of the image.

What are some of the types of frame effects in Elements?

You can give your art a modern look with a **Brushed Aluminum Frame**, create torn edges around your image with a **Spatter Frame**, or add tabbed corners with the **Photo Corners Frame**. You can scroll down in the Effects palette to see all the frame choices available.

How do I give my photo a frame that has a custom color?

Apply the **Foreground Color Frame** effect. This applies a frame using the color currently in the foreground color box.

Add a Fancy Background

You can add a fancy background to your image with one of Elements' several texture effects.

1. Open the Layers palette.

2. Open the Styles and Effects palette.

Note: For more information on opening and using palettes, see Chapter 1.

3. Click the layer above which you want to add the fancy background.

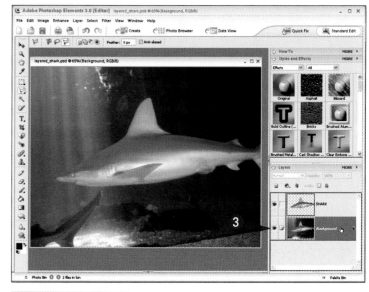

4. Click here and then click **Textures**.

   The texture effects display.

⑤ Double-click an effect.

● You can scroll down to view other effects in the palette.

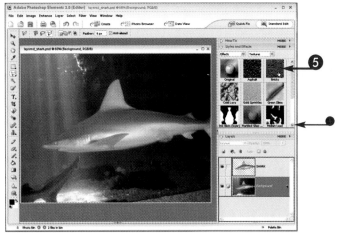

● Photoshop Elements creates a new layer with the texture.

You can click and drag the new layer up or down in the Layers palette to rearrange its position in your image.

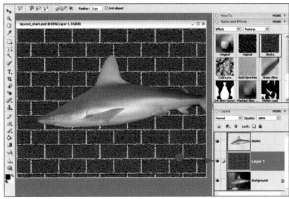

How can I make content underneath a texture effect show through?

Select the layer that contains the effect and then adjust the opacity for that layer. Reducing the opacity to less than 100% allows content underneath the effect to show through.

Is there an easy way to preview what each effect will look like?

You can open the Styles and Effects palette menu and click **List View** to change how you view the options in the palette. When you select an effect, List View displays two generic thumbnails that show how an image appears before and after applying the effect.

Add Beveling to a Layer

You can bevel a layer to give objects in your image a three-dimensional look.

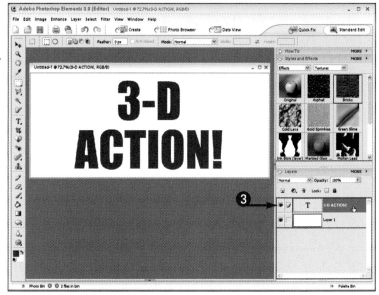

Add Beveling to a Layer

① Open the Layers palette.

② Open the Styles and Effects palette.

Note: For more information on opening and using palettes, see Chapter 1.

③ Click the layer to which you want to apply beveling.

In this example, a text layer is beveled.

Note: For more information about using text, see Chapter 12.

④ Click here and then click **Layer Styles**.

⑤ Click here and then click **Bevels**.

The bevel styles display.

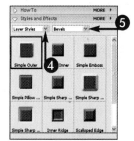

6 Click a bevel style.

● You can scroll down to view other styles in the palette.

Photoshop Elements applies the beveling to the layer.

7 Double-click 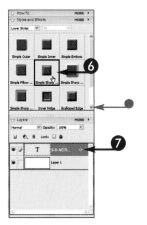 in the affected layer.

The Style Settings dialog box opens.

8 Click and drag the **Lighting Angle** dial to set the direction of the beveling.

9 Click and drag 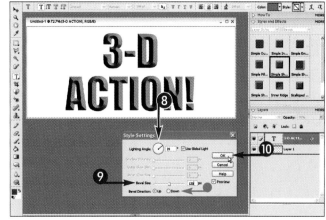 to increase or decrease the bevel size.

● You can click here (○ changes to ◉) to set the bevel direction.

10 Click **OK**.

Photoshop Elements applies the style settings.

TIPS

When would I use the bevel style?

You may find this effect useful for creating three-dimensional buttons for Web pages. For example, to create such a 3D button, you can apply beveling to a colored rectangle and then lay type over it. See Chapter 10 for details about drawing shapes.

How can I remove a style from a layer after I have applied it?

In the Layers palette, you can right-click (Control) click on a Mac) the affected layer, and then click **Clear Layer Style** (you can also click **Layer**, **Layer Style**, and then **Clear Layer Style**). Photoshop Elements removes the style from the layer.

Add an Outer Glow to a Layer

The outer glow style adds faint coloring to the outside edge of a layer, which can help highlight it.

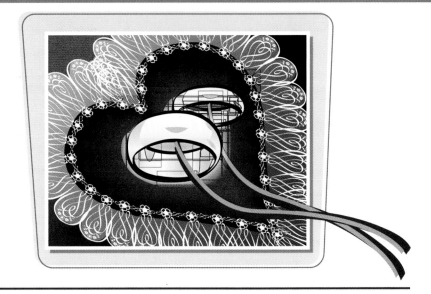

Add an Outer Glow to a Layer

① Open the Layers palette.

② Open the Styles and Effects palette.

Note: *For more information on opening and using palettes, see Chapter 1.*

③ Click the layer to which you want to apply the outer glow.

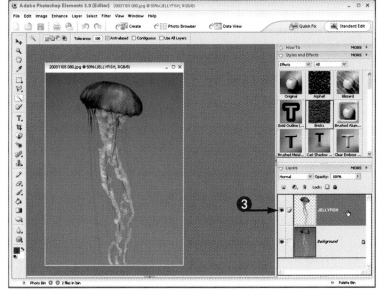

④ Click here and then click **Layer Styles**.

⑤ Click here and then click **Outer Glows**.

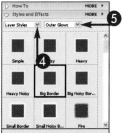

The outer glow styles display.

6 Click an outer glow style.

● You can click and scroll down to view other styles in the palette.

Photoshop Elements applies the outer glow to the layer.

7 Double-click ▓ in the affected layer.

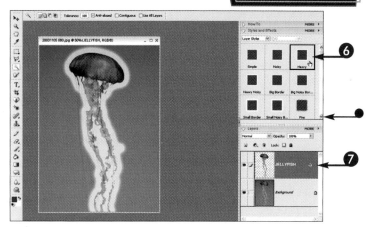

The Style Settings dialog box opens.

8 Click and drag ▢ to increase or decrease the Outer Glow size.

9 Click **OK**.

Photoshop Elements applies the style settings.

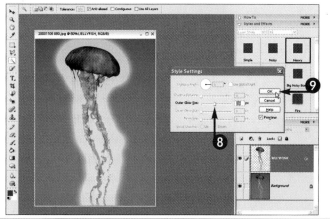

 TIP

Can I add an inner glow to layer objects?

Yes. An inner glow adds color to the inside edge of a layer object. To add this effect:

1 Click a layer.

2 Open the Styles and Effects palette.

Note: For more information on opening and using palettes, see Chapter 1.

3 Click here and then click **Layer Styles**.

4 Click here and then click **Inner Glows**.

5 Click an Inner Glow style.

Photoshop Elements applies the inner glow.

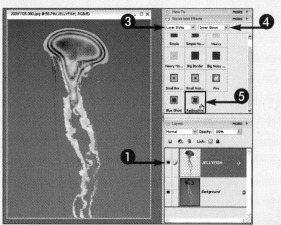

Add a Fancy Covering to a Layer

You can apply any of a variety of layer effects that can make a layer look as if it is covered in colorful metal or glass.

Add a Fancy Covering to a Layer

COVER WITH METAL

① Open the Layers palette.

② Open the Styles and Effects palette.

Note: For more information on opening and using palettes, see Chapter 1.

③ Click the layer that you want to cover.

④ Click here and then click **Layer Styles**.

⑤ Click here and then click **Wow Chrome**.

A number of metallic styles display.

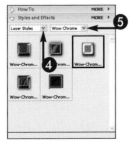

6 Click a style.

Photoshop Elements applies the style to the layer.

COVER WITH GLASS

7 Click the layer that you want to cover.

8 Click here and then click **Glass Buttons**.

9 Click a glass button style.

Photoshop Elements applies the style to the layer.

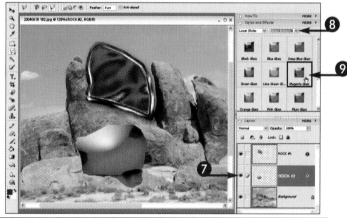

TIP

Is there another method to change the way styles affect my layers?

You can scale the intensity of applied styles by doing the following:

1 Click the layer.

2 Click **Layer**.

3 Click **Layer Style**.

4 Click **Scale Effects**.

The Scale Layer Effects dialog box appears.

5 Type a value to scale the effects from 1% to 1000%.

6 Click **OK** to apply the effect.

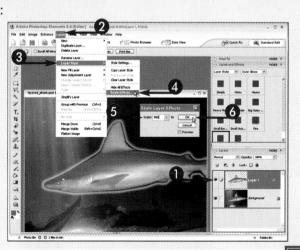

Automating Your Work

Sometimes you want to perform the same simple sequence of commands on a lot of different images. With Elements' image-processing commands, you can automatically convert the file type or change the size of every image file in a folder. Other Photoshop Elements features make it easy to automatically create picture packages and contact sheets.

Convert File Types **244**

Convert Image Sizes **246**

Add Watermarks **248**

Print a Contact Sheet **250**

Print a Picture Package **252**

Convert File Types

You can convert all the image files in a folder to a specific file type. You may find this useful if you want to post a number of pictures on the Web and need the images in a Web file format, such as GIF or JPEG.

Before you can begin, you need to create a source folder and a destination folder for your images in Windows. On a Mac, you create the necessary folder as you convert the files. To work with folders, see your specific operating system's documentation.

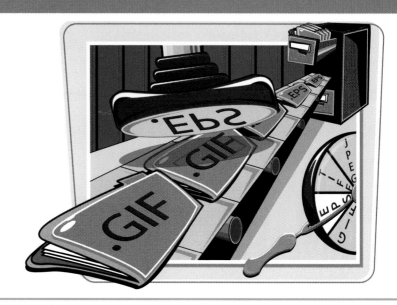

Convert File Types

① Place the images you want to convert into a source folder.

② Create an empty destination folder in which to save your converted files.

③ In Elements, click **File**.

④ Click **Process Multiple Files**.

The Process Multiple Files dialog box opens.

⑤ Click **Browse**.

In Windows, the Browse for Folder dialog box appears. On a Mac, the Choose a folder for processing multiple files dialog box appears.

⑥ In Windows, click ⊞ to open folders. On a Mac, click the folder name to view its contents.

⑦ Click the folder containing your images.

⑧ Click **OK** (**Choose** on a Mac).

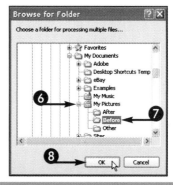

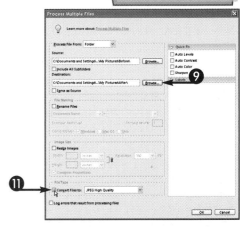

9 Click **Browse**.

In Windows, the Browse for Folder dialog box opens. On a Mac, the Choose a destination folder dialog box appears.

10 Repeat steps **6** to **8** to select the folder where you want the converted files saved.

11 Click the **Convert Files** to option (☐ changes to ☑).

12 Click here and then click a file type to which you want to convert.

13 Click **OK**.

Photoshop Elements cycles through the image files in the source folder.

Elements converts the image files and saves the new versions in the destination folder.

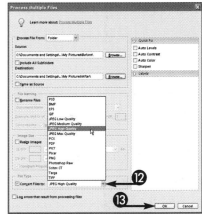

 TIP

How do I rename the image files that I convert?
You can rename files using settings in the Process Multiple Files dialog box:

1 Click the **Rename Files** option (☐ changes to ☑).

2 Click here to select a naming scheme.

Naming options let you include serial numbers or dates in the new file names.

3 If you include a serial number in the naming scheme, type the starting number.

● Elements displays an example of what the name of the converted file will look like.

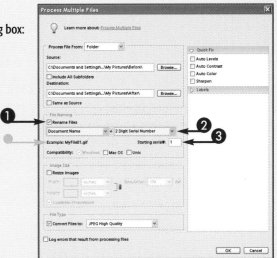

Convert Image Sizes

You can resize all the image files in a folder to specific dimensions. You may find this useful if you want to quickly convert a number of large files from a digital camera to smaller versions that you can store more efficiently and send via e-mail.

Before you can begin, you need to create a source folder and a destination folder for your images in Windows. On a Mac, you create the necessary folder as you convert the files. To work with folders, see your specific operating system's documentation.

Convert Image Sizes

① Place the images you want to resize into a source folder.

② Create an empty destination folder in which to save your resized files.

③ In Elements, click **File**.

④ Click **Process Multiple Files**.

The Process Multiple Files dialog box opens.

⑤ Click **Browse**.

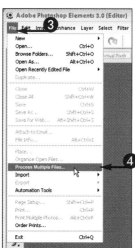

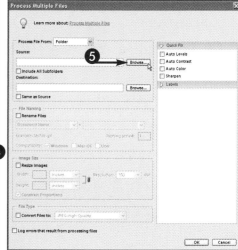

In Windows, the Browse for Folder dialog box opens. On a Mac, the Choose a folder for processing multiple files dialog box appears.

⑥ In Windows, click ⊞ to open folders. On a Mac, click the folder name to view its contents.

⑦ Click the folder containing your images.

⑧ Click **OK** (**Choose** on a Mac).

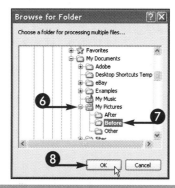

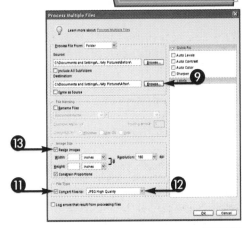

9 Click **Browse**.

In Windows, the Browse for Folder dialog box opens. On a Mac, the Choose a destination folder dialog box appears.

10 Repeat steps **6** to **8** to select the folder where you want to save the resized files.

11 Click the **Convert Files to** option (☐ changes to ☑).

12 Click here and select a file type to save the resized files.

13 Click the **Resize Images** option (☐ changes to ☑).

14 Click here and select the units.

15 Type a value for a dimension.

16 Click the **Constrain Proportions** option (☐ changes to ☑) to size the other dimension automatically.

● You can click here to select a new resolution.

17 Click **OK**.

Photoshop Elements resizes the image files and saves the new versions.

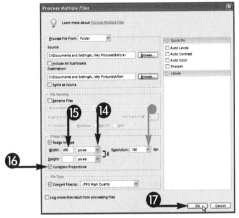

Can I process files that I currently have open in Elements?

Yes. In the Process Multiple Files dialog box, just click the Process Files From box and select **Opened Files**. Photoshop Elements saves the processed files to the destination folder.

How can improve the appearance of photos as I process them?

You can open the Quick Fix palette on the right side of the Process Multiple Files dialog box and have Elements optimize the levels, contrast, and color of each processed photo, and also add sharpening. For more about Quick Fix features, see Chapter 7. For more about sharpening, see Chapter 11.

Add Watermarks

Photoshop Elements can automatically add watermarks to a collection of photos. Watermarks are semi-opaque words or designs overlaid on images to signify ownership and discourage illegal use.

Before you can begin, you need to create a source folder and a destination folder for your images in Windows. On a Mac, you can create the necessary folder as you convert the files. To work with folders, see your specific operating system's documentation.

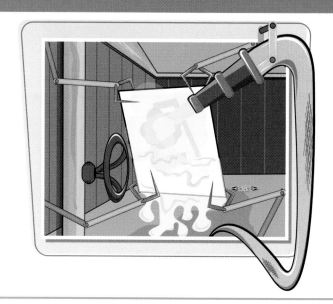

Add Watermarks

① Place the images to which you want to add watermarks into a source folder.

② Create an empty destination folder in which to save your watermarked files.

③ In Elements, click **File**.

④ Click **Process Multiple Files**.

The Process Multiple Files dialog box opens.

⑤ Click **Browse**.

In Windows, the Browse for Folder dialog box opens. On a Mac, the Choose a folder for processing multiple files dialog box appears.

⑥ In Windows, click ➕ to open folders. On a Mac, click the folder name to view its contents.

⑦ Click the folder containing your images.

⑧ Click **OK** (**Choose** on a Mac).

⑨ Click **Browse** and repeat steps **6** to **8** for the destination folder.

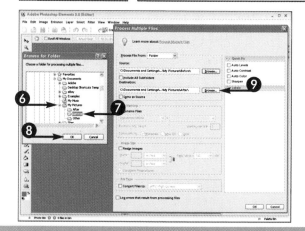

⑩ Click to open the Labels palette.

⑪ Click here and then select **Watermark**.

⑫ Type your watermark text.

⑬ Select the position, font, and size for the text.

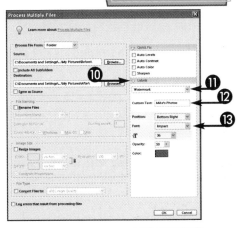

⑭ Click here and specify an opacity from 1 to 100. The lower the opacity, the more transparent the watermark will be.

⑮ Click the color box and select a watermark color.

You may want to select a color that contrasts with the colors in your photo.

⑯ Click **OK**.

Photoshop Elements adds watermarks to the photos in the source folder and saves them in the destination folder.

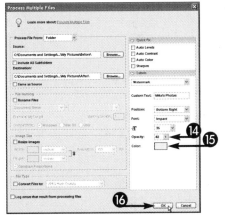

TIPS

How can I automatically add captions to my photos?

In the Process Multiple Files dialog box, you can select Caption under the top menu in the Labels palette. With Caption chosen, Elements applies text that is associated with the photo to the botton-left, -right, or -center of the photo. For more about specifying caption information for a photo, see Chapter 15. Similar to applying a watermark, you can specify the positioning, font, size, opacity, and color of the caption.

What are the different types of captions that I can add to my photos?

You can add the filename, date modified, and description as a caption. You can add this information by itself — for example, just the filename — or in combination by clicking one or more options (☐ changes to ☑).

Print a Contact Sheet

The Elements Organizer can automatically print a photographer's contact sheet. Useful for keeping a hard-copy record of your digital images, contact sheets consist of miniature versions of images and often include ownership information.

① Open the photos you want to print on the contact sheet.

② Click **File**.

③ Click **Print Multiple Photos**.

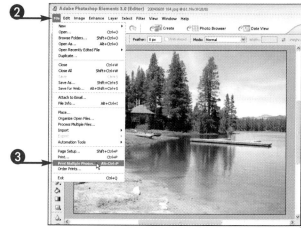

The Organizer opens and the Print Photos dialog box appears.

④ Click here and select a printer.

⑤ Click here and select **Contact Sheet**.

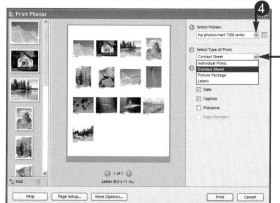

6 Click here and select the number of columns.

7 Click options (☐ changes to ☑) to display labels below each thumbnail image.

Note: For more about setting up captions for your photos, see Chapter 15.

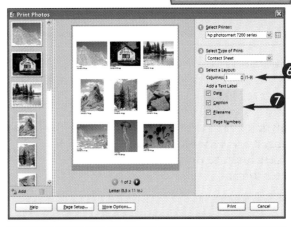

8 Click Print.

Photoshop Elements prints the contact sheet.

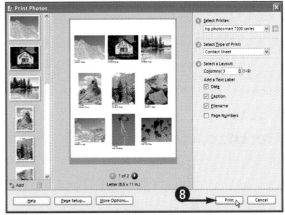

TIP

How do I print a contact sheet on a Mac?

1 Click **File**, and then click **Contact Sheet II** to open the Contact Sheet II dialog box.

2 Click **Choose**.

3 In the Select Image Directory dialog box that opens, navigate to and select the folder containing the images you want, and then click **Choose**.

4 Set any contact sheet properties by typing values and/or clicking the appropriate options.

5 Click **OK** to print your contact sheet.

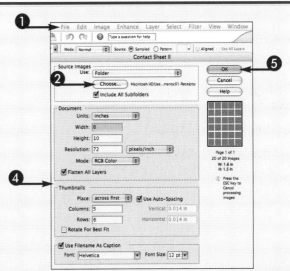

Print a Picture Package

You can automatically create a one-page layout with a selected image at various sizes using the picture package command. You may find this useful when you want to print out pictures for friends, family, or associates.

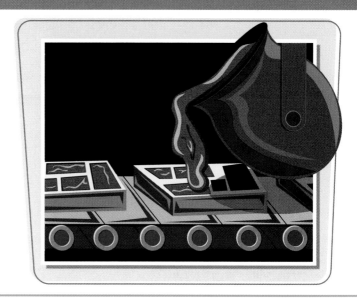

① Open the photo you want to print as a picture package.

② Click **File**.

③ Click **Print Multiple Photos**.

The Organizer opens and the Print Photos dialog box appears.

④ Click here and select a printer.

⑤ Click here and select **Picture Package**.

6 Click here and select a layout.

7 Click here and select a frame.

8 Deselect this option to have Elements print your
   photo multiple times on a page (☑ changes to ☐).

9 Click Print.

   Photoshop Elements prints the picture package.

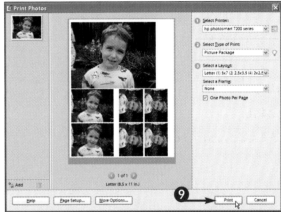

TIP

How do I print a picture package on a Mac?

1 Click **File**; then click **Picture Package**.

2 In the Picture Package dialog
   box that appears, click **Choose**.

3 In the Select an Image File dialog box that appears, navigate
   to and select the image you want, and then click **Open**.

4 Click here to select a page size and a layout.

● You can click individual thumbnails in the layout preview
   to change the image file displayed in that position.

5 Click **OK** to display the picture package.

15

Organize Photos with Organizer

Are you ready to organize your digital photos? PC users can catalog, view, and sort photo files using the Organizer program. Organizer is a separate program that works with Photoshop Elements to help you manage your growing library of digital pictures. This chapter shows you how to take advantage of Organizer's many photo management features.

Introducing Organizer 256

Open Organizer 258

Navigate the Organizer Workspace 260

Catalog Photos Stored on Your
     Computer 262

Catalog Photos from Your Camera 264

Create a New Catalog...................................266

Open a Catalog 268

View Photos in the Photo Browser 270

View Photos by Date....................................272

Review Photos as a Slide Show....................274

Edit a Photo 276

Delete a Photo 277

Work with Tags...278

Group Photos into a Collection 282

View Photo Properties 284

Add a Caption 286

Find a Photo...288

Backup Photos..290

Create a Slide Show Creation 292

You can use the new Organizer program to manage your growing library of digital photos. Whether you scan in your photos, acquire them from another folder on your computer, or upload them directly from your digital camera or card reader, you can use Organizer to view the images. Organizer works alongside Photoshop Elements to help you track and organize your photos.

Virtual Browser

Organizer acts as a virtual browser, enabling you to view thumbnails, or miniature versions of your pictures. The thumbnails you see in Organizer are merely "pointers" to the original file location. The images remain intact in their original location unless you decide to delete them. Organizer enables you to view your many photos from one convenient window. See the sections "View Photos in the Photo Browser" and "View Photos by Date" to learn more.

Get Photos

You can import photos into Organizer using a variety of methods. The Get Photos command enables you to acquire photos from a camera, card reader, scanner, or file system. You can also transfer photos from a mobile phone or online sharing service. After you bring the photos into Organizer, you can view, sort, and categorize them as you like. See the sections "Catalog Photos Stored on Your Computer" and "Catalog Photos from Your Camera" to learn more.

Catalog

When you bring photo files into Organizer, the program adds them to your catalog of images. Images are cataloged by date. You can keep all of your photos in one catalog, or you can store them in separate catalogs. You can also create a catalog for each user on your computer. See the section "Create a New Catalog" and "Open a Catalog" to learn more.

Views

You can view your photos in Organizer by date or by thumbnail view. Organizer includes a timeline you can use to view different batches of photos, and you can choose to view details below each thumbnail. You can also review your images using the Photo Review feature. This turns your catalog into a slide show and you can view a full-screen version of each photo file in sequence. See the section "Review Photos as a Slide Show" to learn more.

Tags

You can use tags to help you sort and track your photos. A tag is a keyword identifier you assign to a photo. After you assign tags, you can then sort through your catalog for pictures matching a certain tag. You can assign any of the preset tags that come with Organizer, or you can create your own. Organizer's presets include tags for people, family, friends, places, and more. You can also assign multiple tags to the same photo. See the section "Work with Tags" to learn more.

Creations

You can turn any photo in your catalog into a creation. For example, you can create custom slide shows of your photos to distribute to friends and family. You can also create photo albums, DVDs, greeting cards, calendars, and more. See the section "Create a Slide Show Creation" to learn more. Also see Chapter 16 to find more tasks to help you turn photos into projects.

Open Organizer

If you are a PC user, you can organize and manage your digital photos in the new Organizer program. Organizer works alongside Photoshop Elements to help you keep track of the growing number of digital photos you store on your computer. You can open Organizer from the Photoshop Elements window or from the Welcome screen that appears when you first start Photoshop Elements.

OPEN ORGANIZER FROM THE WELCOME WINDOW

① Click **Start**.

② Click **All Programs**.

③ Click **Adobe Photoshop Elements 3.0**.

The Photoshop Elements Welcome window, also called the *launcher*, opens.

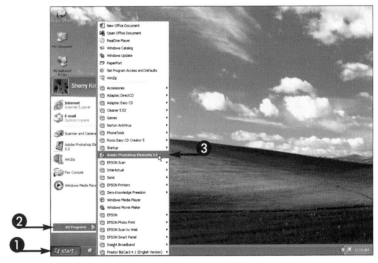

The Welcome window displays clickable shortcuts to common Elements tasks.

④ Click **View and Organize Photos**.

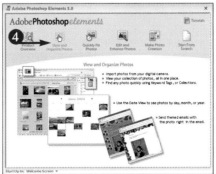

The Organizer program window opens.

Note: *If you have not added any photos to your catalog yet, the Photo Browser appears empty. See the next sections for more on adding photos to your catalog.*

- To open the Photoshop Elements window for editing, click the **Edit** button and then click **Go to Standard Edit**.

Note: *You may need to click a photo before activating the **Edit** button to open Photoshop Elements.*

OPEN ORGANIZER FROM THE PHOTOSHOP ELEMENTS WINDOW

1. Click the **Photo Browser** button.

- You can also click the **Date View** button to open Organizer and view photos by date.

  The Organizer program window opens.

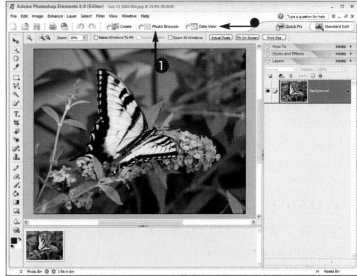

Can I tell Photoshop Elements to open Organizer first every time?

Yes. You can specify whether you want to view the Welcome Screen when you start the program, or jump right to the Photoshop Elements or Organizer windows. To set up Organizer to start automatically, follow these steps:

1. Start Photoshop Elements as you normally do.

2. When the Welcome Screen displays, click the Start Up In ⬇.

3. Click **Organizer**.

   The next time you open Photoshop Elements, Organizer opens automatically.

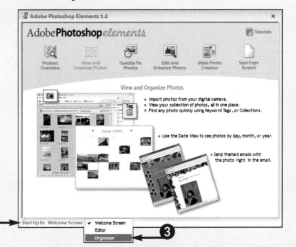

The Organizer window includes a toolbar of buttons
representing common commands and tasks, as well as
areas for viewing and working with photos. Take a
moment and familiarize yourself with the program
window and its elements.

Menu Bar
Displays menu
commands to activate
Organizer features
and tasks.

View Buttons
Use these buttons to switch
between viewing
thumbnails of your photos
or viewing images by date.

Help
You can type a help
keyword or click the Help
icon to access the Organizer
Help files.

Toolbar
Displays buttons for
activating common
Organizer commands
and tasks.

Timeline
Displays a timeline of
your photos. You can
move back and forth
on the timeline to
view photos by dates.

Photo Browser
Displays thumbnails
of your photos. You
can click an image to
select it for editing.

**Photo Browser
Arrangement**
You can click this
menu to change
how photos are
arranged in the
Photo Browser area.

Details
Displays details about
the image, such as the
creation date.

Status Bar
Displays the number of items selected,
the total number of photos and dates,
as well as View Notification and e-mail
buttons for downloading the latest
information from Adobe.

Tag Icon
Tags help you to mark
images for sorting and
tracking by assigning
identifying keywords.

Organizer Bin Display
Click here to hide or display the Organizer bin.

This pane contains two palettes you can use to help you organize your photos. You can click a palette tab to switch between working with tags and collections.

Single Photo View
Click this option to view a selected photo in the Photo Browser.

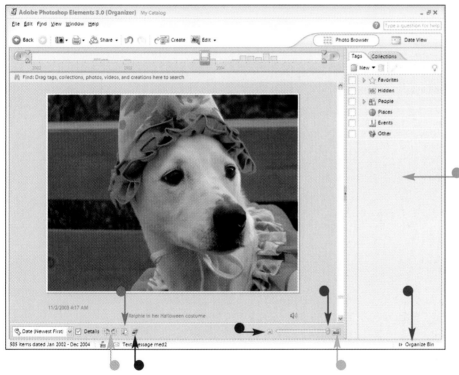

View Slider
You can adjust the size of the thumbnail previews by dragging this slider.

Small Thumbnail Size
Click this option to make the Photo Browser area display small thumbnails of your photos.

Photo Review
Click this button to activate the photo review feature and view your photos as a slide show.

Rotation Buttons
You can use the rotation buttons to change positioning of a photo.

Properties
Use this feature to view properties of a photo, such as the photo file size, creation date, and location.

Catalog Photos Stored on Your Computer

You can add pictures to Organizer to start creating a catalog of digital photos. You can locate image files stored in folders on your computer and import them into Organizer. Organizer catalogs the images and displays thumbnails of the photos. The actual image files remain in their original locations. The thumbnails you see in Organizer merely reference the original photos.

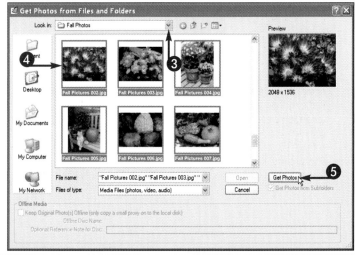

① Click **Get Photos**.

② Click **From Files and Folders**.

You can also import images from a camera, scanner, mobile phone, or online service.

The Get Photos from Files and Folders dialog box appears.

③ Navigate to the folder or drive containing the images you want to catalog.

④ Click the image or images you want to import.

You can press and hold the **Shift** or **Control** key to select multiple images.

⑤ Click **Get Photos**.

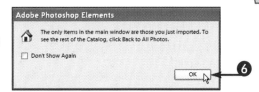

Organizer imports the photos.

A prompt box appears with instructions for viewing the newly acquired files.

⑥ Click **OK**.

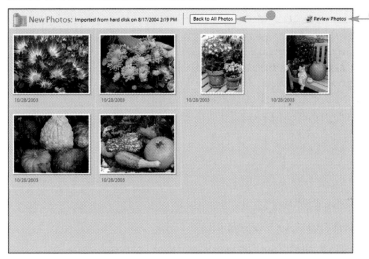

Organizer displays thumbnails of the photos in the Photo Browser.

● You can click **Back to All Photos** to return to your main catalog.

● To review the photos as a slide show, you can click the **Review Photos** button.

Note: *See the section "Review Photos as a Slide Show" for more on the Review Photos feature.*

Can I save the files I edit in Photoshop Elements to my Organizer catalog?

Yes. When you click **Save** or **Save As** in Photoshop Elements, the Save As dialog box offers an option to include the file in your Organizer catalog. Simply click the **Include in Organizer** option (☐ changes to ☑) before you activate the Save button. See Chapter 2 for more on saving edited photos in Photoshop Elements.

How do I catalog photos from a CD or DVD?

You can add photos stored on other media to your catalog by telling Organizer where to search for the photos. You can do this by selecting the storage device in the Look In drop-down list in the Get Photos from Files and Folders dialog box. For example, if your photos are on a CD, insert the CD into your computer's CD drive and select the drive from the Look In list.

Catalog Photos from Your Camera

If you use a digital camera, you can transfer photos from the camera into Organizer. Whether your camera connects directly to your computer, or you use a card reader to transfer images from a storage disk, you can import the photos into Organizer to view and sort.

1 Plug in your camera or card reader and memory card.

2 Click the Get Photos button (📷▾).

3 Click **From Camera or Card Reader**.

You can also import images from a scanner, mobile phone, online service, or from folders on your computer.

Note: See the previous section for more on importing files from your computer. See Chapter 2 to import images from a scanner.

The Get Photos from Camera or Card Reader dialog box appears.

4 Click here and then click your camera or card reader.

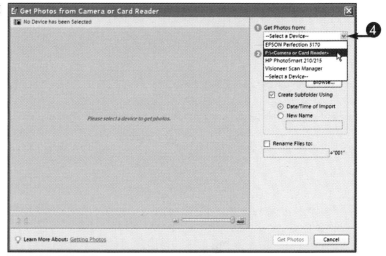

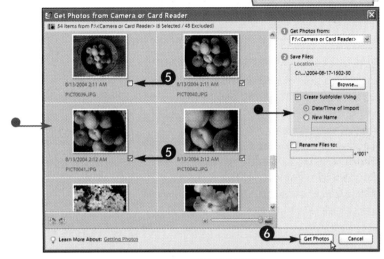

- The stored images appear here.

5 Click to select or deselect the images you want to import (☐ changes to ☑ or ☑ changes to ☐).

A check mark (☑) indicates the image is selected for import.

- To create a folder into which you store images, click the **Create Subfolder Using** option (☐ changes to ☑), click **New Name** (○ changes to ◉), and then type a name for the folder.

6 Click **Get Photos**.

Organizer displays a message box about the imported images.

7 Click **OK** to continue.

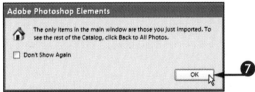

Organizer asks if you want to delete the selected images from the camera or card reader.

8 Click **Yes** to delete or **No** to leave the images on the camera or storage card.

The Organizer window displays the imported images.

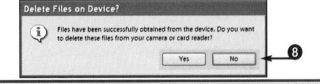

How do I save the photos to a specific folder?

When transferring images from a camera or memory card, you can specify a folder to store in the images in the Get Photos from Camera or Card Reader dialog box. Follow these steps:

1 Click **Browse**.

The Browse for Folder dialog box opens.

2 Navigate to the folder where you want to save the images.

- To create a new folder, click here and type a folder name.

3 Click **OK**.

Continue with step **6** in this section to complete the transfer of images from your camera or memory card.

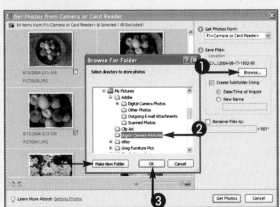

Create a New Catalog

The photos you manage in Organizer are stored in catalogs. You can keep your photos in one large catalog or separate them into smaller catalogs. Organizer stores photos in a catalog file assigning a special file format, called Photoshop Elements Catalog or PSC. You can create numerous catalogs in Organizer to suit the way you want to manage your digital photos.

Create a New Catalog

① Click **File**.

② Click **Catalog**.

The Catalog dialog box appears.

③ Click **New**.

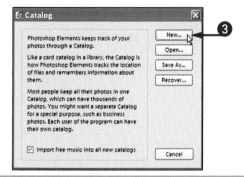

④ Type a name for the new catalog.

By default, Organizer stores catalog files in the Catalog folder, a subfolder found in the Documents and Settings folder.

You can save the catalog file to another folder, if needed.

⑤ Click **Save**.

Organizer opens a new blank catalog.

Note: *See the sections "Catalog Photos Stored on Your Computer" and "Catalog Photos from Your Camera" for more on populating your catalog with images.*

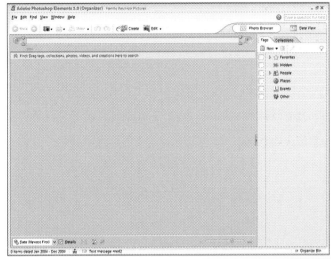

TIPS

Where can I see the name of my current catalog and the number of photos it contains?

Organizer displays the name of the current catalog in the program window's title bar, to the right of the program name. You can quickly see how many photos are within the catalog by looking at the bottom of the program window, in the status bar. The status bar displays the total number of images and the range of dates from the first photo to the most recent photo.

How do I rename an existing catalog?

You can rename a catalog from within the New Catalog or Open Catalog dialog boxes. Make sure the catalog you want to rename is closed. Organizer does not let you rename the current catalog. Click the **File** and then **Catalog** to open the Catalog dialog box, and then click **New** or **Open**. From the dialog box that appears, you can click the catalog name to highlight the file, and then click again and type a new name for the file. When you click outside the filename, Elements applies the new name.

Open a Catalog

If you use more than one catalog to manage your photos, you can open different catalogs to work with various photos. By default, every time you open the Organizer program window, Organizer opens the last catalog you worked on. To open a different catalog, you must use the Open Catalog dialog box.

1 Click **File**.

2 Click **Catalog**.

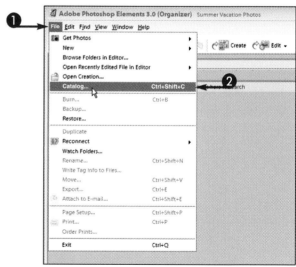

The Catalog dialog box appears.

3 Click **Open**.

The Open Catalog dialog box appears.

④ Click the name of the catalog you want to view.

● You can click here to navigate to another folder and catalog file if you store catalogs in another location.

⑤ Click **Open**.

Organizer opens the specified catalog.

Note: See the sections "Catalog Photos Stored on Your Computer" and "Catalog Photos from Your Camera" for more on populating your catalog with images.

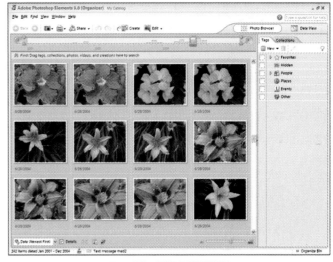

 TIP

Can I group photos together without starting a new catalog?

Yes. You can group related photos or a combination of photos into collections within a catalog. For example, if your catalog contains a year's worth of photos, you can group your vacation pictures or family reunion pictures as a collection. To view only those pictures, you can open the collection in the Photo Browser to see the images. The photos still remain part of the larger catalog, but placing them into a collection can make them easier to find later. See the section "Group Photos into a Collection" for more on this feature.

View Photos in the Photo Browser

As you start adding image files to your catalog, you can view the images using Organizer's Photo Browser. The Photo Browser can display thumbnail, or miniature versions of your photos, or you can display a single image.

① Click the **Photo Browser** button, if the Photo Browser is not already displayed.

② Click and drag the Timeline slider (■) to the month you want to view.

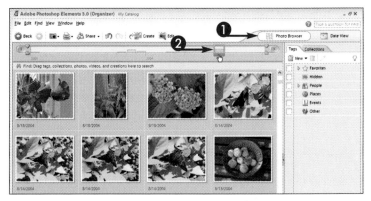

The Photo Browser displays the photos for that particular month.

③ Click and drag the View Slider ▣.

Click and drag ▣ to the left to make the thumbnails smaller.

Click and drag the ▣ to the right to make the thumbnails larger.

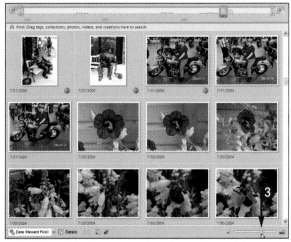

Organizer adjusts the size of the thumbnail images.

● You can use the scroll bars to scroll through the images.

● You can click this option to turn details on or off.

④ Click a photo to select the image.

⑤ Click the Single Photo View button ().

Photo Browser displays the selected photo.

● You can click here to type a caption for the photo.

● To change the view arrangement options, you can click here and then select another arrangement.

What view arrangements can I apply?

You can use the Photo Browser Arrangement menu to change how you view your catalog in the Photo Browser. You can view photos by oldest first, newest first, the latest imported batch, or by folder location. By default, Organizer displays newest photos first in the Photo Browser.

How do I rotate a sideways image in the Photo Browser view?

To rotate a sideways image, first click the image in the Photo Browser and then click the Rotate Left or Rotate Right buttons ( )at the bottom of the window. Organizer immediately corrects the photo's orientation.

View Photos by Date

To help you keep track of your photos, Organizer organizes the images by date. You can use the Date View mode to view photos by their dates. With Date View, you can view a calendar showing the dates you imported photos into your catalog. You can then view the images for that particular day as a slide show.

① Click the **Date View** button.

Organizer displays a calendar view of your catalog.

② Click a date view option.

You can view your photos by year, month, or day. In this example, the Month view is displayed.

● To view a different month, click the Previous Month (⊙) or Next Month (⊙) buttons to scroll to the month you want to view.

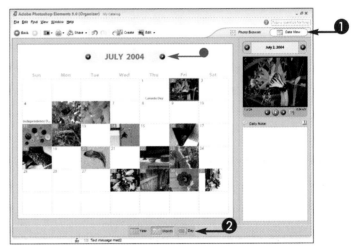

③ Click the date for the photos you want to view.

● The first photo in the group appears here.

In Day view, the first photo appears in place of the calendar.

④ Click the Play button (⊙).

Organizer starts the automatic sequencing feature, displaying each slide from the date you selected.

- To pause or stop the sequencing, click the Pause button ().

  To view the previous image again, click the Previous Item button ().

  To view the next image, click Next Item ().

- To add a note about the day's photos, click here and type your text.

- To view the current photo in the Photo Browser, click .

Daily Note:

These photos were taken in the backyard in late afternoon light

---

TIP

What is the difference between the three date view options?

Year View

You can use this view to see the dates displayed as a yearly calendar.

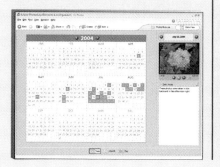

Month View

Use this view to see your catalog as a monthly calendar.

Day View

You can use this view to see a day's catalog of photos.

Review Photos as a Slide Show

After you bring photos into Organizer you can view them as a slide show. The Photo Review feature displays your photos as full-screen images on your computer screen. A toolbar at the top offers navigational buttons to advance each photo, as well as tools for changing the view.

The Photo Review feature installs with several music files you can use as background music for your slide show. You can also use music files stored on your computer as background music.

Review Photos as a Slide Show

① Click the **Review Photos** button in Photo Browser view.

Note: See the section "View Photos in the Photo Browser" for more on the Photo Browser.

● If the button is not visible, you can click **View** and then click **Photo Review**.

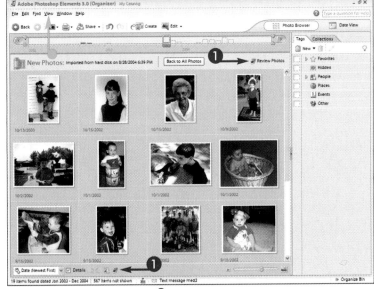

The Photo Review dialog box appears.

② Set any presentation options you want to assign.

● To select different background music, or none at all, click here and click a selection.

● If you have a music file you want to play with the slide show, click **Browse** and select the file.

● Click here to set a length for each slide here.

③ Click **OK**.

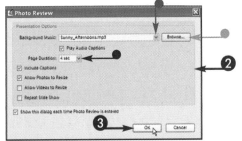

Photo Review displays the first slide in the series as well as a toolbar.

④ Click the Play button ().

Photo Review starts the slide show and advances each slide automatically.

To advance the slides manually, click the Next Photo (⬤) or Previous Photo (⬤) buttons.

● You can click the Rotate buttons to fix a sideways image.

● You can also click a specific photo to display.

● Click here to show only the navigational controls.

⑤ Click the Exit button (⬤).

The slide show stops and you return to the Organizer window.

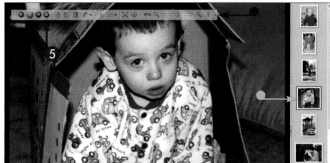

TIP

What do the other tools do on the navigation toolbar?

🔲 🔲	**Rotate** Click the Rotate Left or Rotate Right buttons to change the orientation of a photo.
🔲	**Delete** Click the Delete button to remove the photo from the catalog.
🔲 ▾	**Action Menu** Click the Action menu to display a menu of tasks, such as tagging the photo or marking it for printing.
🔲 🔲 ▾	**Review Modes** Click a review mode button to view a single photo in the slide show or compare two photos side by side.
🔲 🔲	**Image Size** Click one of these buttons to view the photo at actual size or sized to fit in the window.
33% 🔍 ━━●━━ 🔍	**Zoom Controls** You can click a zoom button or drag the zoom ◯ to change the magnification setting of the image.
🔲	**Sync Pan and Zoom** Synchronizes the panning and zooming operations of Complex Slideshows to create a smoother transition.

You can edit a photo in Organizer by switching over to the Photoshop Elements editor window, or you can edit directly in Organizer with the Auto Fix window. The Auto Fix offers several key editing tools, such as Auto Levels.

Edit a Photo

① Click the photo you want to edit in the Photo Browser.

You can also edit the current photo in Date View.

② Click the **Edit** button.

③ Click **Auto Fix Window**.

If you click **Go to Quick Fix** or **Go to Standard Edit**, the Photoshop Elements editor window opens.

Note: See Chapter 7 to read about the Quick Fix feature.

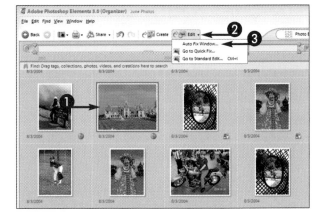

The Auto Fix window opens.

④ Click the edit you want to perform.

● A preview of the edit appears here.

● You can click here to crop the image.

● You can drag the 🔲 to zoom your view in or out.

⑤ Click **OK**.

Organizer applies the changes.

Note: See Chapters 7 to 9 to read more about photo editing techniques.

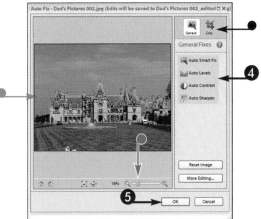

You can delete a photo you no longer need from the Organizer catalog. For example, you may want to delete duplicate photos, or photos too blurry to keep. Deleting the reference in Organizer does not delete the file in its original location.

Delete a Photo

① Click the photo you want to remove in the Photo Browser.

② Press **Delete**.

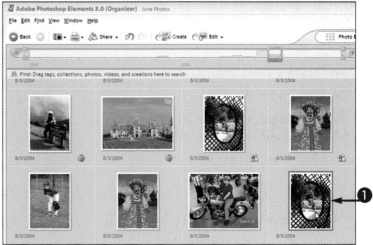

A Confirm Deletion from Catalog box appears.

③ Click **OK** to delete the photo from the catalog.

● To permanently delete the photo from your computer as well, click this option (☐ changes to ☑).

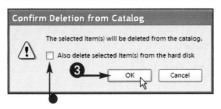

Work with Tags

You can use tags to help you categorize and sort your digital photos. You can assign Organizer's preset tags, or you can create your own tags. You can also assign more than one tag to a photo.

Preset tags include tags for people, family, and friends. You can assign tags to categories and subcategories.

CREATE A NEW TAG

① Click the Tags palette if it is not already displayed in the Organizer bin.

② Click the **New** button.

③ Click **New Tag**.

The Create Tag dialog box appears.

④ Click here and then click a category for the new tag.

⑤ Type a name for the tag.

● You can add a note about the tag here.

⑥ Click **OK**.

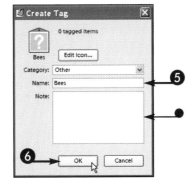

ASSIGN A TAG

⑦ Click and drag the tag from the Tags palette and drop it on the photo you want to tag.

Organizer assigns the tag.

You can use the same drag-and-drop technique to assign preset tags as well as tags you create.

● A tag icon indicates the photo has a tag assigned.

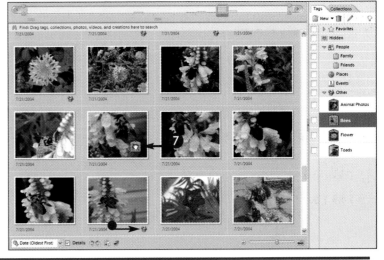

TIP

How do I edit a tag name?

① Right-click over the tag in the Tags palette tab and click the **Edit Tag** command.

This opens the Edit Tag dialog box.

② Type the tag name or assign a new category to the tag.

③ Click **OK**.

Organizer applies the changes.

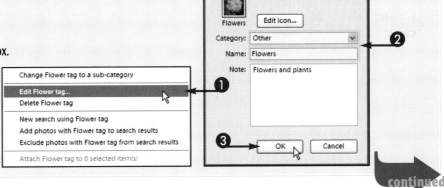

continued

After you assign tags, you can sort your catalog by tags. For example, you can sort your photos to show only pictures of people or events. You can sort on two or more categories. You can also remove a tag you no longer want assigned to a photo.

Work with Tags *(continued)*

SORT BY TAGS

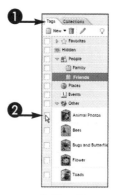

① Click the Tags palette if it is not already displayed.

② Click the check box in front of the tag you want to sort (☐ changes to ☑).

Click the ▷ to expand a tag category.

Click the ▽ to collapse a tag category.

You can sort more than one tag by selecting the other tags you want to include in the search.

● Organizer adds a Find icon (🔍) to the box.

● Organizer immediately displays all the photos sharing the specified tag.

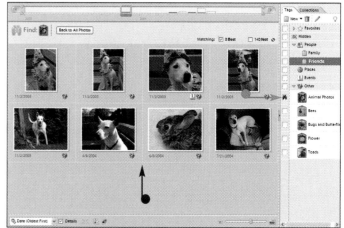

REMOVE A TAG

1 Right-click the photo containing the tag you want to remove.

2 Click **Remove Tag**.

3 Click the tag you want to remove.

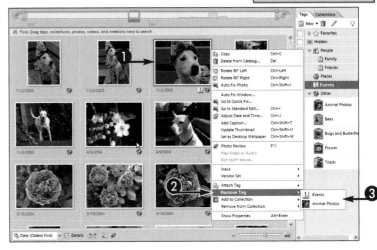

● Organizer removes the tag.

How do I attach the same tag to multiple photos?

1 In the Photo Browser, click the photos you want to tag.

You can press and hold the Ctrl key to select multiple photos.

2 Right-click over one of the selected photos, and click **Attach Tag to Selected Items**.

3 Click the tag category and tag name you want to assign.

Organizer assigns the tags.

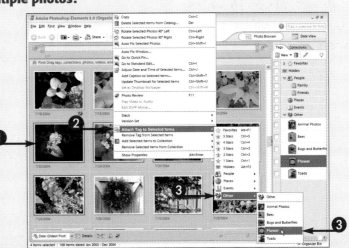

Group Photos into a Collection

You can use collections as another way to organize your photos. For example, you may group related photos together and assign them a unique name. Adding similar or related photos to a collection makes it easier to locate the photos at a later time.

CREATE A NEW COLLECTION

1. Display the photos you want to add to a collection in the Photo Browser.

Note: See the section "View Photos in the Photo Browser" for more.

2. Click the **Collections** palette in the Organizer bin.

3. Click the **New** button.

4. Click **New Collection**.

The Create Collection dialog box opens.

5. Type a name for the collection.

- You can assign the collection to a group, if desired.

- Optionally, you can add a note about the collection here.

6. Click **OK**.

Organizer adds the new collection to the Collections palette.

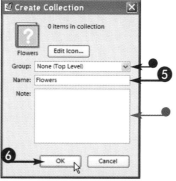

ASSIGN A PHOTO TO A COLLECTION

7 Click and drag the photo from the Photo Browser and drop it on the collection label.

Organizer adds the photo to the collection.

You can also click and drag the collection label in the Organizer bin and drop it over the photo in the Photo Browser.

To add multiple images to a collection, press and hold the **Shift** or **Control** key while clicking photos and then drag the photos as a group to the Collection palette.

VIEW A COLLECTION

8 Click the check box in front of the collection you want to view.

Organizer displays all the photos within the collection.

● Photos assigned to a collection are marked with a Collection icon.

● You can click the Back button (⊙) or **Back to All Photos** to return to the catalog.

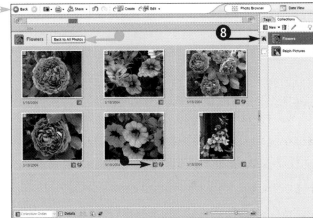

How do I remove a collection?

Removing a collection does not remove the images from the Organizer catalog, it simply removes the image group. To remove a collection you no longer need, follow these steps:

1 Click the collection you want to remove in the Collections palette.

2 Click the Delete button (🗑).

Organizer displays a message box concerning the deletion.

3 Click **OK**.

Organizer removes the collection.

View Photo Properties

You can view the properties for any photo in your catalog. You can use the Properties box to view a photo's general information, which includes the filename, file size, image size, and location. You can also view any associated tags, file history, and metadata information. Metadata, or EXIF data, is detailed information about how the photo was taken, including the camera settings, such as exposure time and F-stop.

1 Click a photo.

2 Click the Show or Hide Properties button (📷).

The Properties box opens.

● The General information appears by default.

● You can view information about the file size and the image size here.

● To view a list of associated tags, click the **Tags** button.

③ Click the **History** button.

● The Properties box displays the file history for the image.

④ Click the **Metadata** button.

The Properties box displays detailed camera information about the image, also called the EXIF data.

● You can click and drag the border to resize the box to view all the information.

⑤ Click the Show or Hide Properties button (🖼).

Organizer hides the Properties box.

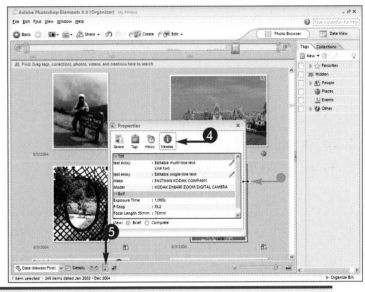

TIP

How do I change the photo's date and time?
To change the date and time associated with a photo, follow these steps:

① Right-click on the photo you want to edit.

② Click **Adjust Date and Time**.

The Adjust Date and Time dialog box opens.

③ Click the **Change to a specified date and time** option (◯ changes to ◉).

④ Click **OK**.

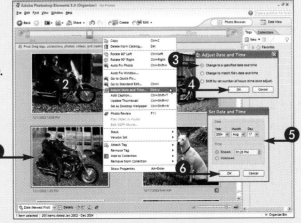

⑤ In the Set Date and Time dialog box, set the new date and time data you want to assign.

⑥ Click **OK**.

Organizer assigns the information and adjusts the photo's placement in the catalog based on the new information.

Add a Caption

You can add captions to your photos to help you remember important information about the images you catalog. For example, you may add captions to your vacation pictures with details about the location or subject matter. Captions appear below a photo when viewing the image in a Photo Review slide show or in Single Photo View.

Add a Caption

① Right-click on the photo you want to caption.

② Click **Add Caption**.

The Add Caption dialog box appears.

③ Type a caption for the photo.

④ Click **OK**.

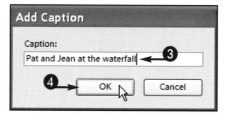

Organizer adds the caption to the photo.

5 Click .

● The caption appears below the photo.

Note: For more on viewing photos in the Photo Browser, see the section "View Photos in the Photo Browser" earlier in this chapter.

● In Photo Review, the caption appears on the slide.

Note: For more on reviewing photos as a slide show, see the section "Review Photos as a Slide Show."

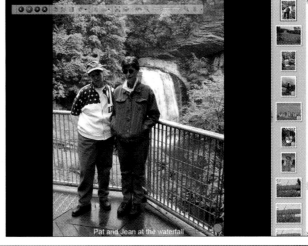

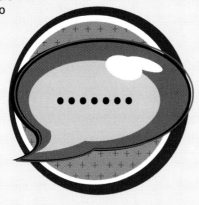

Are there other ways to add captions to my photos?

Yes. You can also add captions to your photos through the Properties box. See the section "View Photo Properties" for more on displaying the box. You can type a caption in the Caption text box.

How do I edit or delete a caption?

To remove a caption you no longer want, view the photo in Single Photo View in the Photo Browser window, click the caption, and make your changes. You can delete the caption completely, type a new caption, or make changes to the existing caption text. Press Enter (Return) to complete your changes.

Find a Photo

Organizer offers a variety of methods you can use to find a particular photo in your catalog. You can search for photos by date, filename, tags, and more. In this section, you search by setting a date range and by searching for a particular file range. Be sure to investigate the other types of search options listed in the Find menu to conduct other types of searches through your catalog.

Find a Photo

① Click **Find**.

② Click **Set Date Range**.

The Set Date Range dialog box opens.

③ Type or click and select the start date for the date range you want to search.

④ Type or click to set the end date for the date range you want to search.

⑤ Click **OK**.

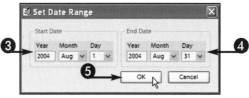

● Organizer displays any matching photos in the Photo Browser and narrows the Timeline parameters to the designated range.

You can view only the photos within the selected date range.

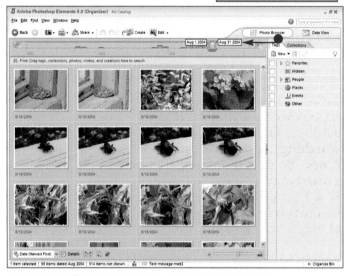

6 Click **Find**.

7 Click **Clear Date Range**.

Organizer resets the Timeline to include all the dates again.

 TIP

What other search methods can I employ?

Other Search Methods

By Caption or Note	Looks for photos based on text content that you add to the notes and captions of a photo.
By Filename	Searches the catalog for a particular filename.
By History	Looks up a photo based on when it was printed, e-mailed, or imported.
By Media Type	Searches for creations, photos, audio, and video files in your catalog.
Items with Unknown Date or Time	Looks for photos lacking date or time data.
By Color Similarity with Selected Photos	Finds photos that appear similar to a selected photo.
Untagged Items	Searches for photos without assigned tags.
Items not in any Collection	Displays items not associated with any collection.

Backup Photos

You can backup your collection of digital photos using Organizer's Burn/Backup Wizard. This feature walks you through the steps for backing up your photo files to a CD or DVD, or another storage device.

Backup Photos

① Open the catalog you want to backup.

Note: See the section "Open a Catalog" to read more.

② Click **File**.

③ Click **Backup**.

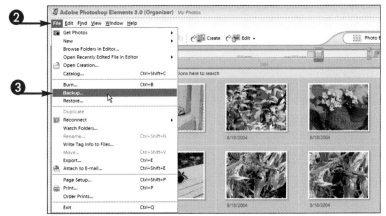

The Burn/Backup wizard opens.

④ Click the **Backup the Catalog** option (○ changes to ◉).

You can also use this same dialog box to burn copies of your photos to a CD or DVD to share with friends and family.

⑤ Click **Next**.

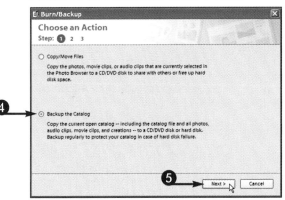

6 Click the **Full Backup** option (○ changes to ●).

● For subsequent backups, you can select the **Incremental Backup** option (○ changes to ●).

7 Click **Next**.

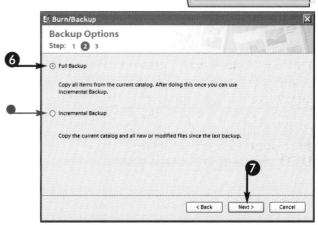

8 Click the drive to which you want to copy the backup files.

● You can type a name for the backup in this text box.

● Depending on your backup drive selection, the wizard displays an estimated file size and creation time.

9 Click **Done**.

Organizer begins backing up your photos.

When the procedure is complete, a prompt box appears to alert you. Click **OK**.

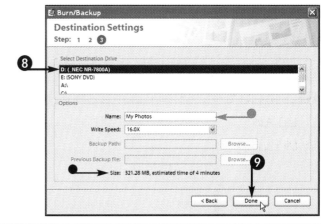

Organizer prompts me to find missing files before backing up my photos. What do I do?

If any of the catalog photos no longer contain valid links to their original files, Organizer may display a prompt box asking you to reconnect any missing files. Missing files can occur if you move the original file after you add the photo to Organizer. You can click **Reconnect** to allow Organizer to look for the missing links and then continue with the backup when finished.

How do I restore my backed up files?

You can click **File** and then **Restore** to restore backups of your photos onto your computer. The Restore dialog box offers options for restoring backed up photos and catalogs to their original location, or to a new location of your choosing.

Create a Slide Show Creation

You can use the Create feature in Organizer to create a variety of projects using the photos in your Organizer catalog. For example, you can create slide shows and share them with others, or turn your photos into album pages, calendars, and even Web galleries. This section focuses on creating a simple slide show to present to others in a PDF slide show format.

PDF slide shows are easy to share with others by copying the finished file onto a disk or e-mailing it to the recipient.

1 Click the **Create** button.

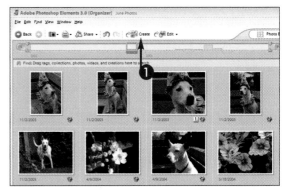

The Creation Setup dialog box opens.

2 Click the **Slide Show** creation.

If you select another type of creation, different dialog boxes will open to help you complete your project.

3 Click **OK**.

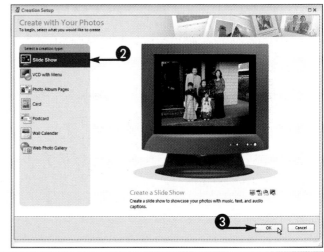

④ Click the Simple Slide Show.

You can create a more complex show with the Custom Slide Show option.

⑤ Click **OK**.

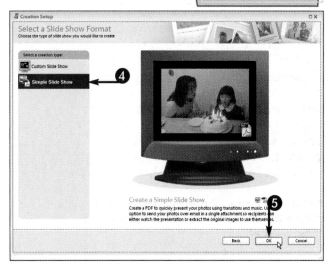

The Simple Slide Show dialog box opens.

If you selected the Custom Slide Show, a similar dialog box opens.

⑥ Click the **Add Photos** button.

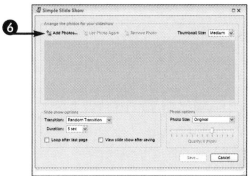

How do I add music to my slide show?

To add music or narration to a slide show, select the Custom Slide Show type from the Creation Setup dialog box. With a custom show, you can add music, record your own narration, add pan and zoom effects, and more. Organizer supports MP3, WAV, and WMA audio file formats. The Create feature includes a built-in audio recorder you can use to record your own narration for the slides.

What other types of creations can I make with my photos?

You can use the Create feature to create a VCD, a video compact disk, of photos, photo album pages, a greeting card using your photo as the illustration, a postcard, a wall calendar, and a Web photo gallery. VCDs can play full motion video and sounds as well as display images. When you click the **Create** button, you can select the project you want to make. Each project involves a different set of dialog boxes that lead you through the creation process. See Chapter 16 for more on outputting your images with Organizer.

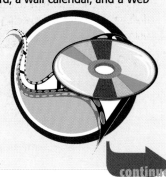

continued

Create a Slide Show Creation *(continued)*

When creating a slide show, you can control the transition effects, slide duration, and even set the show to loop continuously. Slide transition effects control how one slide transitions to the next slide.

Organizer saves your slide show as a PDF file. PDF files are a popular file format read by Adobe Acrobat Reader.

Create a Slide Show Creation *(continued)*

The Add Photos dialog box appears.

⑦ Click to select the photos you want to include in the show (☐ changes to ☑).

● You can add photos by tags, collection, or include the entire catalog.

⑧ Click **OK**.

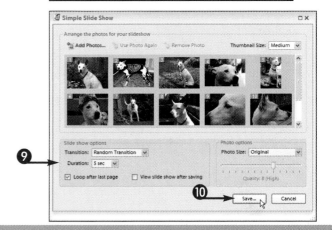

⑨ Set any additional options you want to assign to the show.

You can specify transition effects, timing, and looping for your show.

⑩ Click **Save**.

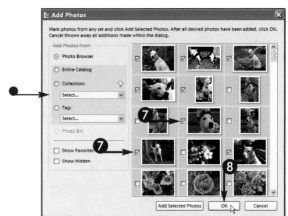

The Save Simple Slide Show dialog box appears.

⑪ Navigate to the folder in which you want to save the slide show file.

⑫ Type a name for the file.

⑬ Click **Save**.

Organizer saves your show.

A prompt box appears announcing your success.

⑭ Click **OK**.

To view the show, double-click the filename.

To exit the show, press Esc.

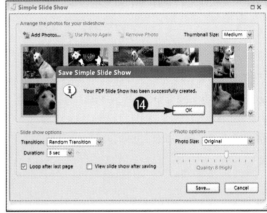

TIPS

<table>
<tr><th>How do I rearrange the photos in my slide show?</th><th>Can I preview my slide show?</th></tr>
<tr><td>In the Simple Slide Show dialog box, shown in step 9 in this section, you can click and drag the photo thumbnails to reposition the order of the slides. To remove a slide entirely, click the slide and click Remove Photo. To add more slides to the show, click the Add Photo button and select additional photos.</td><td>If you click the View slide show after saving option (☐ changes to ☑) in the Simple Slide Show dialog box, you can view the show as soon as you finish saving the file. To preview a show while creating it, use the Custom Slide Show option instead of the Simple Slide Show option. The Photoshop Elements Slide Show Editor window includes navigation buttons you can use to preview the show.</td></tr>
</table>

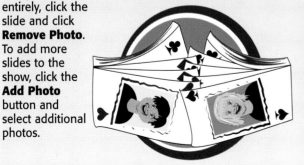

Outputting Images

Do you want to save your files for later use, or so that you can use them on the Web? This chapter shows you how. It also shows you how to print images from a Mac or PC, and how to send your finished images via e-mail.

Add Caption and Copyright Information 298

Save a JPEG for the Web 300

Save a GIF for the Web 302

Preview an Image in a Browser.......................304

Create a Web Photo Gallery on a PC 306

Create a Postcard on a PC.................................310

Send an Image with E-mail on a PC............314

Preview a Printout..316

Print an Image from a PC 318

Print an Image from a Mac..............................320

Add Caption and Copyright Information

You can store caption and copyright information with your saved image. You may find this useful if you plan on selling your images or publishing them online.

Some image editing applications – such as Photoshop Elements – can detect copyright information from an image and display it to a user who opens it.

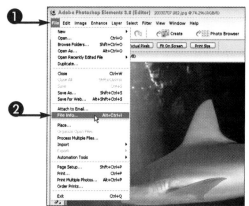

Add Caption and Copyright Information

① Click **File**.

② Click **File Info**.

The File Info dialog box appears.

③ Type caption description and other information for your image.

Note: *Adding tags to your images converts their tag text into keywords. To add keywords to your image and to work with tags on a PC, see Chapter 16.*

Note: *To print the caption description along with the image using settings in the Print Preview dialog box, see the section "Preview a Printout."*

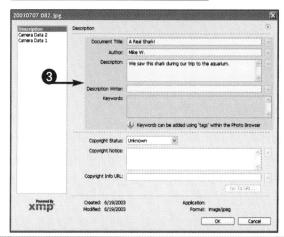

④ Click here and select **Copyrighted**.

⑤ Type a copyright notice.

● You can type a Web address that you want to associate with the image.

⑥ Click **OK**.

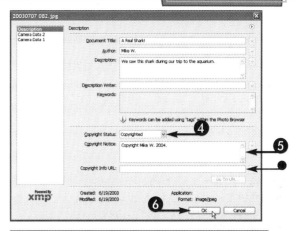

● Photoshop Elements places a copyright symbol in the title bar.

Note: Another way of protecting copyrighted photos is by adding a watermark. See Chapter 14 for details.

Save a JPEG for the Web

You can save a file in the JPEG format — Joint Photographic Experts Group — and publish it on the Web. JPEG is the preferred file format for saving photographic images.

Save a JPEG for the Web

① Click **File**.

② Click **Save for Web**.

The Save For Web dialog box appears.

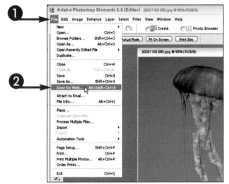

③ Click here and select **JPEG**.

④ Click here to select a JPEG quality setting.

A descriptive setting or a numeric value of 0 is low quality, with 100 being maximum quality; the higher the quality, the larger the resulting file.

⑤ Check that the file quality and size are acceptable in the preview window.

⑥ Click **OK**.

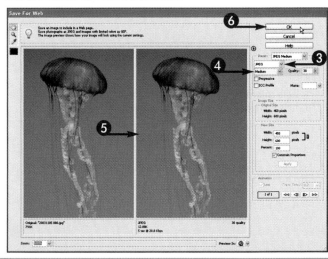

The Save Optimized As dialog box appears.

7 In Windows, click here and select a folder in which to save the file.

On a Mac, select the column view to locate a folder in which to save the file.

8 Type a filename.

9 Click **Save**.

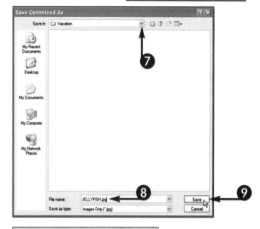

Photoshop Elements saves the JPEG file in the specified folder and you can open the folder to access the file.

● The original image file remains open in Elements.

What is image compression?

Image compression involves using mathematical techniques to reduce the amount of information required to describe an image. This results in small file sizes, which is important when transmitting information efficiently on the Web. Some compression schemes, such as JPEG, involve some loss in quality due to the compression, but the loss is usually negligible compared to the file size savings.

How can I resize an image that I am saving for the Web?

You can resize an image immediately prior to saving it for the Web in the Image Resize area of the Save For Web dialog box. You can change the height and width, or you can change the size by a percentage of the current size.

You can save a file as a GIF — Graphics Interchange Format — and publish it on the Web. The GIF format is good for saving illustrations that have a lot of solid color. The format supports a maximum of 256 colors.

Save a GIF for the Web

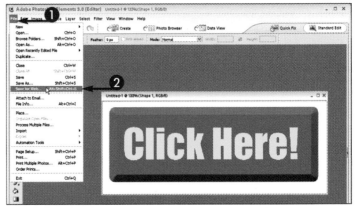

① Click **File**.

② Click **Save for Web**.

The Save For Web dialog box appears.

③ Click here and select **GIF**.

④ Click here and select the number of colors to include in the image.

GIF allows a maximum of 256 colors, making it unsuitable for many photos.

⑤ Check that the file quality and size are acceptable in the preview window.

⑥ Click **OK**.

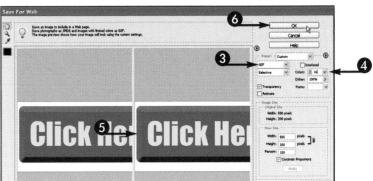

The Save Optimized As dialog box appears.

7 In Windows, click here and select a folder in which to save the file.

On a Mac, select the column view to locate a folder in which to save the file.

8 Type a filename.

9 Click **Save**.

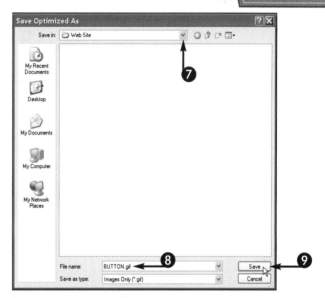

Photoshop Elements saves the GIF file in the specified folder and you can open the folder to access the file.

● The original image file remains open in Elements.

 TIPS

How do I minimize the file sizes of my GIF images?

The most important factor in creating small GIFs is limiting the number of colors in the final image. GIF files are limited to 256 colors or fewer. In images that have just a few solid colors, you can often reduce the total number of colors to 16 or 8 without any noticeable reduction in quality. See step **4** in this section for setting the number of colors in your GIF images.

How can I include transparency in my Web image?

If you are saving your image as a GIF, you can click Transparency in the Save For Web dialog box to preserve any transparent areas of your image in the resulting GIF file. Transparent areas of your Elements image are distinguished by a gray-and-white checkerboard pattern. You cannot include transparency in JPEG images. In JPEGs, transparent areas are automatically filled with the matte color.

Preview an Image in a Browser

You can preview an Elements image in a Web browser to check how the image will display on a Web page. Photoshop Elements lets you preview your image in different browsers installed on your computer.

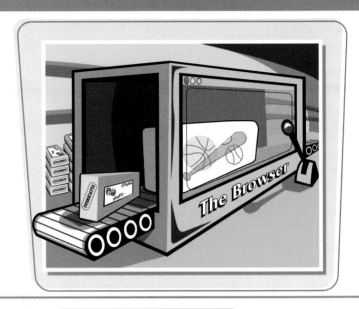

Preview an Image in a Browser

① Click **File**.

② Click **Save for Web**.

The Save For Web dialog box opens.

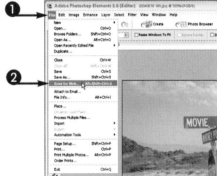

③ Click the **Preview In** button.

Photoshop Elements opens the default Web browser on your computer.

Photoshop Elements displays the image in the browser window.

● General information about the image displays below the image.

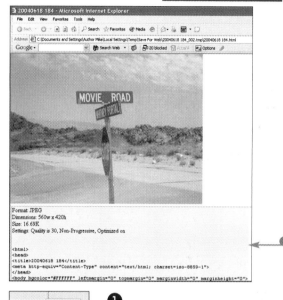

SET THE DEFAULT BROWSER

① Click here and then **Edit List**.

The Browsers window opens.

② Click **Find All**.

● Photoshop Elements populates the list with the browsers installed on your computer.

③ Click a browser name.

④ Click **Set As Default**.

Photoshop Elements sets the browser as the default.

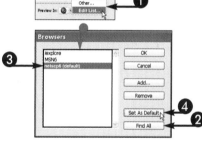

TIPS

How can I create a Web page that displays my image?

Elements displays HTML in the browser window when you preview an image. You can copy the HTML to create a Web page that can display the image. After you save the HTML file in a text editor, you can display the image online by uploading it and the image file to a Web server.

How do you display an image on a Web page using HTML?

You use an IMG tag with an SRC attribute. The SRC attribute tells the Web browser where the image is located on your Web site. For example, this HTML displays an image file named "my-image.jpg" located in a folder named "images":

```
<IMG SRC="images/my-image.jpg">
```

Create a Web Photo Gallery on a PC

On a PC, you can have Photoshop Elements create a photo gallery Web site that showcases your images. Elements not only sizes and optimizes your image files for the site, but it also creates the Web pages that display the images and links those pages together.

You can build a Web photo gallery on a Mac by selecting Create Web Photo Gallery under the File menu.

Create a Web Photo Gallery on a PC

1 Open the Elements Organizer.

Note: For more information about using the Organizer, see Chapter 15.

2 `Ctrl`-click the images that you want to display in your gallery.

If you do not select any photos, Elements displays all of the images in your gallery.

3 Click **File**.

4 Click **New**.

5 Click **Web Photo Gallery**.

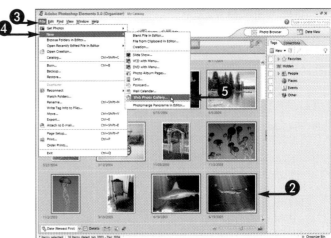

The Adobe Web Photo Gallery dialog box opens.

6 Click a gallery style.

The style determines the gallery theme as well as how the images are organized.

7 Type the title for the gallery banner.

● You can type an optional e-mail address to display in your gallery.

8 Click here to format the gallery title.

9 Click **Browse**.

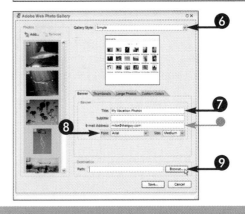

The Browse For Folder dialog box opens.

🔟 Click the folder in which to save your gallery.

⓫ Click **OK**.

The folder appears in the Path field.

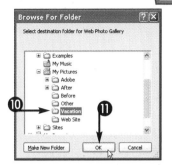

⓬ Click the **Thumbnails** tab.

Thumbnails are the clickable miniature versions of your images in the gallery.

⓭ Click here to specify the size of the thumbnails.

⓮ Click to select formatting for the thumbnail captions.

⓯ Click these options (☐ changes to ☑) to specify what information will appear for the captions.

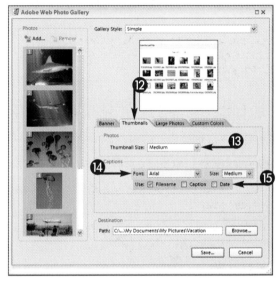

TIPS

How do I determine the number of thumbnails that appear on each photo gallery page?

Photoshop Elements arranges the images on the pages based on the size of the thumbnails. To increase the number of images on each page, select a smaller thumbnail size. To decrease the number of photos on each page, select a larger thumbnail size.

How does the e-mail address appear in my gallery?

Where the e-mail address appears depends on the chosen gallery style. It may appear below the gallery title, or it may appear below each large image. The e-mail address displayed is clickable; clicking it opens a new e-mail message on a viewer's computer.

continued

When you create a Web photo gallery, you specify the size and quality of the images that display in the gallery. Photoshop Elements creates small versions of your gallery images, which viewers can click to access larger versions.

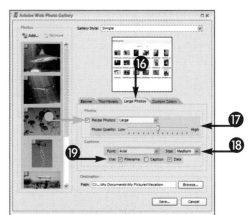

⑯ Click the **Large Photos** tab.

⑰ Click, or drag the 🔘, to set the size and quality of the large photos.

Note: Larger and higher-quality images take longer to download over the Web.

● You can deselect this option (☑ changes to ☐) to keep your images their current size.

⑱ Click these options to specify the formatting of the larger photo captions.

⑲ Click these options (☐ changes to ☑) to specify what information is used for the captions.

⑳ Click the **Custom Colors** tab.

㉑ Click a color box.

The Color dialog box opens.

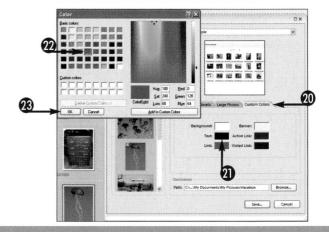

㉒ Click a color.

㉓ Click **OK**.

㉔ Repeats steps **20** and **22** for each color in the gallery.

25 Click **Save**.

Photoshop Elements closes the Adobe Web Photo Gallery window and builds the image and HTML files for the gallery.

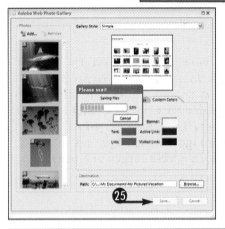

Photoshop Elements opens the completed gallery in a Web Photo Gallery Browser window.

The window displays how the gallery looks in a regular Web browser, such as Microsoft Internet Explorer or Netscape Navigator.

You can click a thumbnail to view a large photo.

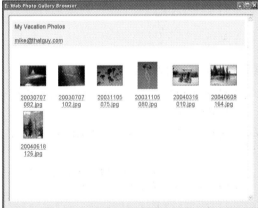

 TIPS

How do I view my Web photo gallery in a regular Web browser?

You can start your Web browser and then open the "index.html" file located in the folder that you specified in step **9**. You can typically click **File** and then **Open** to open a file on your computer with your browser. The "index.html" file represents the home page of your Web photo gallery.

How can I edit the gallery pages after Elements creates them?

After you create your photo gallery, you can use a Web publishing program, such as Macromedia Dreamweaver, or Adobe GoLive, to edit the HTML pages. Or, if you know how to code HTML, you can edit them with a text editor, such as Notepad (on a PC) or TextEdit (on a Mac).

Create a Postcard on a PC

On a PC, you can design a printable postcard using one of your Elements images. Photoshop Elements enables you to decorate your postcard with a variety of border styles. You can also add custom text.

① From the Elements Editor in the Organizer, click **Photo Browser**.

Note: For more information about using the Organizer, see Chapter 15.

The Organizer appears.

② Click an image for the front of your postcard.

③ Click **File**.

④ Click **New**.

⑤ Click **Postcard**.

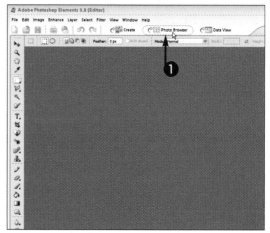

The Creation Set-up window appears.

6 Click a postcard style.

● An example of the style appears.

7 Click **Next Step**.

The Arrange Your Photos pane of the Create a Postcard window appears.

● Clicking **Add Photos** lets you create multiple postcards, each with a different photo.

● Selecting a photo and then clicking **Use Photo Again** lets you duplicate a photo and print it on multiple postcards.

● You can click **Remove Photo** to delete a photo from your postcard project.

8 Click **Next Step**.

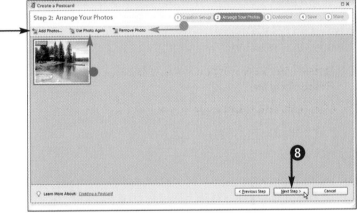

TIPS

How can I create a greeting card?

Creating a greeting card is similar to creating a postcard. You select an image in the Elements Organizer, click **File**, **New**, and then **Card**. Next, you follow the steps to select a card style, add optional text, and then print, save, or e-mail the final product. The Mac version of Elements does not include a greeting card feature. But Mac users can create greeting cards in iPhoto, a Mac-based image organizer and editor.

How can I create a wall calendar?

Creating a calendar is also similar to creating a postcard. For a calendar, you initially select 13 images — one for the calendar cover, and one for each month. Then you click **File**, **New**, and then **Wall Calendar**.

continued

After you create your postcard, you can print it, create a PDF file of it, e-mail it to someone else, or order professionally-made prints of it.

Create and Print a Postcard *(continued)*

The Customize pane of the Create a Postcard window appears.

9 Double-click the postcard text.

A Title dialog box appears.

10 Type title text to appear on the postcard.

● You can select various options to format the text.

11 Click **Done**.

12 Click **Next Step**.

The Save pane of the Create a Postcard window appears.

13 Type a name for the postcard.

● You can click an option (☐ changes to ☑) to use the title text as the name.

14 Click **Save**.

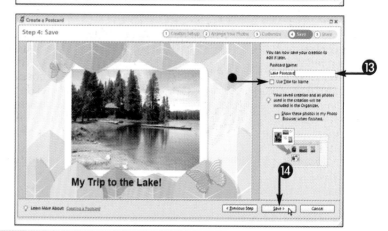

The Share pane of the Create a Postcard window appears.

● Photoshop Elements lets you save or print the new postcard in various ways.

Note: For more information about printing and e-mailing photos, see the other tasks in this chapter.

⓯ Click **Done**.

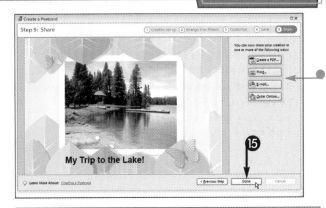

The Organizer appears.

● The new postcard is saved in the main window.

TIPS

What if I do not want text to accompany my postcard?
Some of the postcard styles include generic placeholder text. To get rid of it, you can double-click the text, delete the text in the Title window that appears, and then click **Done**. Your postcard becomes text-free.

Can I reorient or resize the image on my postcard?
In the Customize window, you can click and drag the image to reorient it on the front of the postcard. You can click and drag the image corners to resize it. This is useful if the image is an odd shape, or if you want to include a lot of text on your postcard.

Send an Image with E-mail on a PC

On a PC, you can have Elements attach an image to a message in your computer's e-mail program. This enables you to send your imaging projects to other people who are online.

This feature requires you to already have an e-mail program, such as Microsoft Outlook or Eudora, set up on your computer. Photoshop Elements does not come with e-mail capability.

You can send images with e-mail on a Mac by selecting Attach to Email under the File menu.

Send an Image with E-mail on a PC

❶ From the Elements Editor in the Organizer, click **Photo Browser**.

Note: For more information about using the Organizer, see Chapter 15.

❷ **Ctrl** -click to select the images you want to send.

❸ Click **File**.

❹ Click **Attach to E-mail**.

*Note: Photoshop Elements may display a window asking you to choose your e-mail client. If so, choose the software with which you prefer to send e-mail and click **Continue**.*

The Attach Selected Items to E-mail window opens.

❺ Click **Add Recipient**.

The Add a recipient dialog box appears.

❻ Type the name and e-mail address of the recipient.

❼ Click **OK**.

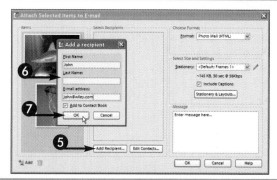

Photoshop Elements adds the recipient to the Select Recipients list and selects it.

8 Click here to select a format for your e-mail.

You can send your images as attachments, embedded in your message (Photo Mail), or as a slide show.

9 Click here to select your custom format settings.

Note: *These settings may differ depending on the chosen format.*

10 Type a message.

11 Click **OK**.

Photoshop Elements opens a new message in your e-mail client software.

● The recipient is added to the "To" field, and your message text is included in the message field.

Note: *For more information about sending your message, see the documentation for your e-mail application.*

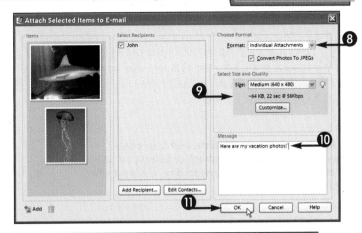

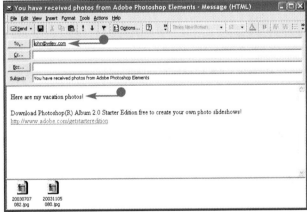

TIP

Can I add different photo templates to my e-mails?
You can access various templates that can add themes to your messages:

1 Click here and select **Photo Mail (HTML)**.

2 Click **Stationery & Layouts**.

3 In the Stationery & Layouts Wizard that appears, click a stationery style to view and the stationery appears in the main window.

4 Click **Next Step**.

When you click **Done** in the window that follows, Elements adds the layout to the e-mail Stationery menu.

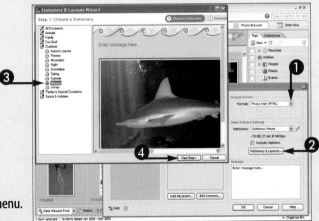

Preview a Printout

Photoshop Elements lets you preview your printout, as well as adjust the size and positioning of your printed image, in the Print Preview dialog box. Previewing lets you check your work without having to actually print on paper.

Preview a Printout

1 Make sure that the layers you want to print are visible.

Note: An 👁 means that a layer is visible. To read more about layers, see Chapter 6.

2 Click **File**.

3 Click **Print**.

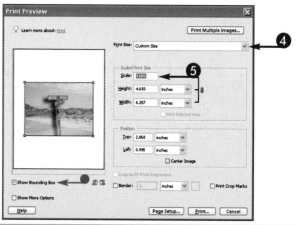

The Print Preview dialog box appears.

4 Click here and then click a print size.

Photoshop Elements offers a variety of standard photo sizes.

5 Type a percentage in the Scale box to shrink or expand the image.

● If the **Show Bounding Box** option is not selected, you can reposition and resize the image by clicking it (☐ changes to ☑).

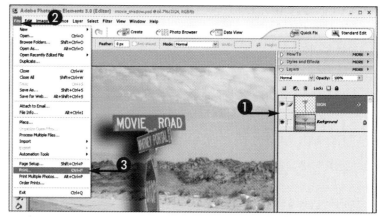

⑥ Click **Center Image** to allow for the repositioning of the image (☑ changes to ☐).

⑦ Click and drag in the image window to reposition the image on the page.

● You can position your image precisely by typing values in the Top and Left fields.

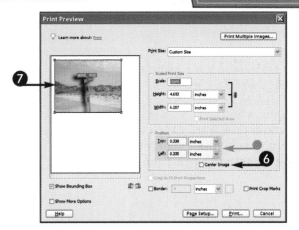

● You can click and drag the handles (☐) on the image edges to scale the image.

⑧ Click **Print**.

● You can click **Cancel** to exit the Print Preview dialog box without printing.

Your image prints.

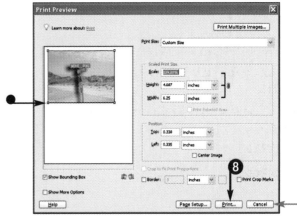

How can I maximize the size of my image on the printed page?

In the Print Preview dialog box, you can click the Print Size ☑ (⊞) and choose **Fit on Page** to scale the image to the maximum size for the current printing settings.

How can I add the filename or a caption to my printed image?

In the Print Preview dialog box, click **Show More Options** (☐ changes to ☑) and then click **Filename** and/or **Caption** (☐ changes to ☑). The filename is printed above the image, the caption below.

Print an Image from a PC

You can print your Photoshop Elements image from a PC computer to create a hard copy of your work.

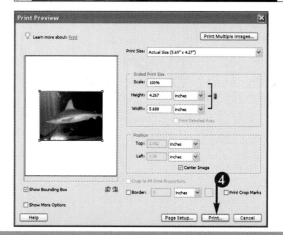

① Make sure that the layers you want to print are visible.

Note: An Eye icon (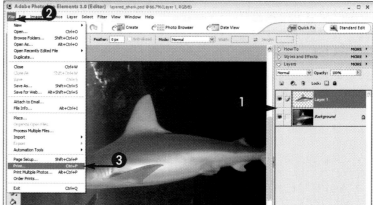) means that a layer is visible. To read more about layers, see Chapter 6.

② Click **File**.

③ Click **Print**.

The Print Preview dialog box appears.

Note: For details on using the Print Preview settings, see the section "Preview a Printout."

④ Click **Print**.

The Print dialog box appears.

5 Click **Properties**.

The Properties dialog box appears.

Note: The Properties dialog box may vary depending on the printer you have selected.

6 Click these options to specify the paper size, print quality, and other settings.

7 Click **OK**.

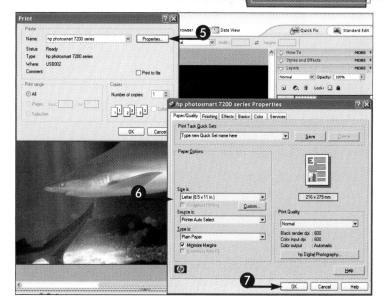

8 Click these options or type values to specify the number of copies and other print settings.

9 Click **OK**.

The image prints.

TIPS

What is the difference between portrait and landscape orientation?

Portrait, which is the default orientation for most printers, prints with the long edge of the page oriented vertically. A standard 8.5-inch by 11-inch sheet of paper measures 11 inches up and down in portrait mode. *Landscape* prints with the paper turned 90 degrees. The long edge of the page is oriented horizontally. You can often specify the orientation in the Properties dialog box when you print a photo.

How can I add extra blank space around my printed image?

You can add a border to the printed image in the Print Preview dialog box. Click the **Border** option (☐ changes to ☑) and select the border size. Photoshop Elements adds blank space around the edge of your image. It displays in the preview box.

Print an Image from a Mac

You can print your Photoshop Elements image from a Mac to create a hard copy of your work.

① Make sure that the layers you want to print are visible.

Note: An 👁 means that a layer is visible. To read more about layers, see Chapter 9.

② Click **File**.

③ Click **Print**.

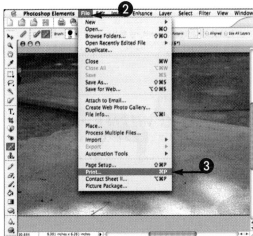

The Print Preview dialog box appears.

Note: For details on using the Print Preview settings, see the section "Preview a Printout."

④ Click **Page Setup**.

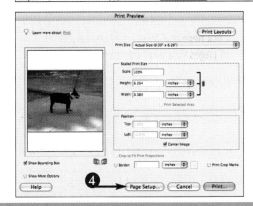

The Page Setup dialog box appears.

⑤ Click these options to specify the printer, paper size, and print orientation.

● You can set a scaling factor by typing a percentage in the Scale text box.

⑥ Click **OK**.

⑦ Click **Print**.

The Print dialog box appears.

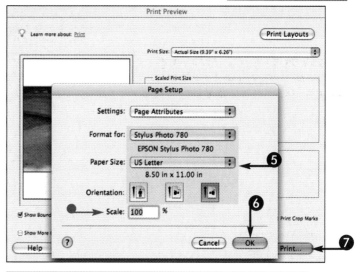

⑧ Click here and then click a printer.

⑨ Type the number of copies you want.

⑩ Click a range of pages you want to print (○ changes to ●) and type a range, if necessary.

⑪ Click **Print**.

Your copies print.

● You can click **Save As PDF** to print to a PDF file rather than a printer or click **Fax** to send your image as a Fax.

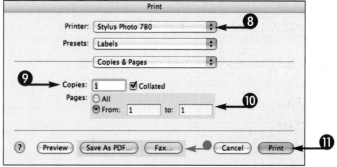

TIP

How do I print multiple pages in Mac OS X?

The Layout option is especially useful in Elements because you can print 2 or 4 pages per sheet to create a greeting card layout. In the Print dialog box:

① Click here and then click **Layout**.

② Click here and then click the number of pages you want per sheet.

③ Click a layout direction option.

④ You can click here to select a border for your printout.

○ You can click **Preview** to preview your layout.

⑤ Click **Print** to print multiple pages.

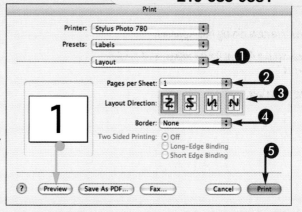

Index

A

Actual Pixels, default image display, 55
Add a Recipient dialog box, e-mail attachments, 314
Add Caption dialog box, 286–287
Add Noise dialog box, add/remove graininess, 206–207
Add Photos dialog box, slide shows, 294
Adjust Date and Time dialog box, 285
Adjustment layers
    blending modes, 121
    create, 118–120
    Multiply blending mode, 172–173
    partial image canvas application, 119
    uses, 101
Adobe GoLive, photo gallery edits, 309
Adobe Online, technical support, 23
Adobe Photo Downloader, image downloads, 38–41
Adobe Web Photo Gallery dialog box, 306–309
alignments, formatted text, 217
animals, green eye corrections, 127
antialising, formatted text, 217
Artistic filters, painted effects, 202–203
attachments, e-mail, 314–315
Auto Color Correction, hue/saturation color corrections, 163
Auto Contrast, photo corrections, 149
Auto Fix Photo, Organizer element, 37
Auto Fix window, photo edits, 276

B

background colors
    Background Eraser tool, 193
    reset to default, 181
    selections, 180–181
Background Eraser tool, photo edits, 193
background layer
    create a layer from, 111
    default bottom layer, 103
    Emboss filter effects, 210–211
    feather selections, 97
    reposition selections, 88–89
    scaled selection result, 93
    selection deletion result, 91
    selection rotation result, 92
    skew selection result, 94
    texture effects, 234–235
backups, photos, 290–291
Bas Relief dialog box, two-toned embossed effect, 211
bevels, layer application, 236–237
bitmap images, file size considerations, 7
black and white photos
    color addition, 176–177
    color photo conversion, 174–175

blank space, add around printed image, 319
Block mode, erasers, 193
Blur filters, image blurs, 198–199
Blur tool
    photo corrections, 158
    Toolbox element, 13
borders
    add blank space around printed image, 319
    selection feather, 96–97
brightness
    automatic adjustments, 145
    Dodge tool adjustments, 150–151
    Equalize filter, 170
    Exposure level adjustments, 151
    level adjustments, 148–149
    pixel point selections, 145
Brightness/Contrast dialog box, photo corrections, 148–149
Browse for Folder dialog box, photo folder selections, 265
browsers
    default selection, 305
    image preview, 304–305
    photo gallery view, 309
Brush mode, erasers, 193
Brush tool
    brush styles, 184–185
    color application, 182–185
    Toolbox element, 13
Brushed Aluminum Frame, image effects, 233
Brushes palette, brush style selections, 165
Burn tool
    green eye (animal) photo corrections, 127
    photo corrections, 152–153
Burn/Backup Wizard, photo backups, 290–291

C

calendars, create, 311
camcorders, video import, 42–43
Camera Data, photo information retrieval, 299
Canvas Size dialog box, 64–65
captions
    automatic addition to photos, 249
    delete, 287
    edit, 287
    output file addition, 298–299
    photo addition, 286–287
    printed image edition, 317
card readers
    Adobe Photo Downloader, 38–41
    image import, 32–33
    Organizer image import, 34–37
Catalog dialog box, 267–269

catalogs
create new, 266–267
name display, 267
open, 268–269
photo deletion, 277
photo groups, 269
photo property views, 284–285
photo searches, 288–289
photo storage information display, 267
photos from cameras, 264–265
photos stored on computer, 262–263
rename, 267
slide show creation, 292–295
CDs, Organizer catalogs, 263
Charcoal dialog box, sketched effect, 204–205
clip art
image acquisition method, 27
image insertion, 49
Clone Stamp tool
photo corrections, 128–129
seamless effects techniques, 129
Toolbox element, 13
collections
new creation, 282
photo assignment, 283
remove, 283
views, 283
color channels, remove color from one color channel, 175
Color Correction palette, photo corrections, 124
color corrections. See also photo corrections
black and white conversion, 174–175
color replacements, 168–169
Color Variations, 166–167
Equalize filter, 170
hue/saturation adjustments, 162–163, 164–165
Multiply blending mode, 172–173
Paint Bucket tool, 169
Posterize filter, 171
Sponge tool, 164–165
Color Picker dialog box, foreground/background color selections, 180–181
Color Variations dialog box, color corrections, 166–167
colors
add to layer part, 117
formatted text, 218–219
frames, 233
GIF format limits, 303
compression, images, 301
contact sheets, print, 250–251
contrast, level adjustments, 148–149

conversions
file types, 244–245
image size, 246–247
Cookie Cutter tool
photo corrections, 136–137
Toolbox element, 12
copyrights, output file addition, 298–299
Create Collection dialog box, new collection creation, 282
Create Tag dialog box, 278–279
Create Texture mode, photo corrections, 130
Creation Setup dialog box, slide show creation, 292–295
Crop tool
photo corrections, 134–135
Toolbox element, 12
versus canvas size adjustments, 65
Crystallize dialog box, colored polygons, 208–209
Custom Shape tool
shapes, 188–189
straight lines, 190
Toolbox element, 13
Cutout filter, painted effects, 203

D

Date View mode, photo views, 272–273
Day View mode, photo views, 273
Delete Selection dialog box, 85
Details, Organizer workspace element, 260
digital cameras
Adobe Photo Downloader, 38–41
image acquisition method, 6, 26
image import, 30–31
Organizer image import, 34–37
photo information retrieval, 299
digital images
acquisition methods, 6, 26–27
Adobe Photo Downloader, 38–41
measurement unit guidelines, 21
Organizer utility, 34–37
pixels, 6
raster versus vector graphics, 7
supported file formats, 7
digital videos
image acquisition method, 6
import, 42–43
directional lights, Lighting Effects filter, 154–155
Distort filters, image distortion, 200–201
documents, scanned image, 29
Dodge tool, photo corrections, 150–151
dots
paint with Brush tool, 185
Pixelate filters, 208–209

Index

draw
  background/foreground color selections, 180–181
  Custom Shape tool, 188–189
  Eraser tool, 192–193
  Gradient tool, 194–195
  image acquisition method, 27
  lines, 190–191
  resize shape, 189
  Sketch filters, 204–205
  strokes, 191
drop shadows
  image effects, 228–231
  layer application, 230–231
  text effects, 225
Dry Brush filter, painted effects, 202
Duplicate Image dialog box, duplicate an image, 67
Dust & Scratches dialog box, photo corrections, 132–133
DVDs, Organizer catalogs, 263

E

Edit Mode tabs, Windows PC/Macintosh workspace, 9, 11
Edit Tag dialog box, tag edits, 279
effects, 229. *See also* Styles and Effects palette
Elliptical Marquee tool, image selections, 71
e-mail
  image attachments, 314–315
  templates, 315
e-mail address, photo gallery display, 307
Emboss filters, three-dimensional shapes, 210–211
emphasis
  formatted text, 216–217
  Sharpen/Blur tool corrections, 158–159
Enhance menu, photo correction commands, 125
Equalize filter, color corrections, 170
Eraser tool
  photo edits, 192–193
  Toolbox element, 13
exposure
  overexposure correction, 157
  underexposure correction, 156–157
Exposure level, brightness adjustments, 151
Eyedropper tool, Toolbox element, 12

F

Feather Selection dialog box, 96–97
File Browser
  card reader image import, 32–33
  hide/display, 33
file formats
  layered files, 101
  supported types, 7, 44, 47
File Info dialog box, caption/copyright information, 298–299

filenames, printed image addition, 317
files
  backup restore, 291
  conversion, 244–245
  rename files, 245
  supported types, 7, 44, 47
Fill Layer dialog box, entire layer/selection color fill, 187
fill layers, create, 116–117
Filter Gallery dialog box, painted effects, 202–203
filters
  Add Noise, 206
  Artistic, 202–203
  Bas Relief, 211
  Blur, 198–199
  Brightness/Contrast, 148–149
  Charcoal, 204
  Crystallize, 208
  Cutout, 203
  Distort, 200–201
  Dry Brush, 202
  Emboss, 210–211
  Equalize, 170
  formatted text application, 220–221
  Gaussian Blur, 159, 198–199
  Invert, 153
  Lens Flare, 155
  Lighting Effects, 154–155, 201
  Liquify, 200
  Mosaic, 209
  Motion Blur, 199
  Neon Glow, 221
  Noise, 206–207
  Photocopy, 205
  Pixelate, 208–209
  Posterize, 171
  Ripple, 221
  Shadows/Highlights, 146–147
  Sketch, 204–205
  Sponge, 203
  Stylize, 210
  Twirl, 201
  Unsharp Mask, 140–141, 159, 201
  Watercolor, 203
  Zig Zag, 201
flash, Lens Flare filter, 155
flatten, layers, 101
fonts, formatted text, 216–217
Foreground & Background tool, Toolbox element, 13
Foreground Color Frame, custom color application, 233
foreground colors
  reset to default, 181
  selections, 180–181